P9-CFM-607

Published in 1999 by Artisan
A Division of Workman Publishing Company, Inc.
708 Broadway, New York, NY 10003–9555
www.workmanweb.com

Printed in China

10   9   8   7   6   5   4   3   2   1

First Printing

Photo Editor: Lori Hogan
Designer: Robbin L. Gourley

FRONT COVER:
Western Tanager, Scarlet Tanager

BACK COVER:
Say's Phoebe, Western Kingbird, Scissor-tailed Flycatcher

by John James Audubon

AUDUBON LIFE·LIST JOURNAL

NATIONAL AUDUBON SOCIETY

ARTISAN   NEW YORK

Contents

Foreword

AN ESTIMATED sixty-five million people—one out of every three adults—in the United States enjoy feeding and watching backyard birds. Birds are a familiar part of our everyday lives. In autumn, two billion to five billion birds initiate long southward journeys, navigating with pinpoint accuracy. In spring, as the days lengthen and the foliage thickens, we watch them hurry back to reach breeding areas and lay claim to their territories.

As you use this book to enhance your enjoyment of birds, keep in mind that migratory birds are the common property and the common responsibility of many nations. Their numbers and populations mirror the health of the global environment. Birds are sensitive indicators of biological richness and diversity and give us a lens through which we can view environmental trends.

New evidence indicates that many bird populations are showing signs of stress and points to major long-term declines in some species' numbers. These trends have serious implications for the rest of the environment. The precipitous decline of such grassland-nesting species as the Dickcissel and the Henslow's Sparrow, for instance, is due in part to the loss of all but one percent of the United States's native tall-grass prairie, along with increasing degradation of the birds' wintering habitats in Central and South America. Similarly, the continuing drop in wading-bird populations has gone hand in hand with the destruction of more than half of this country's original wetlands.

These problems must be addressed through cooperative efforts, both national and international, to change the policies and actions that bear on the quality and extent of avian habitats. The National Audubon Society has a long history of bird conservation, and we hope you will join us in our effort to ensure that future generations will be able to admire the rich diversity of bird life, including the species featured in this book.

John Flicker
President
National Audubon Society

How to Use This Book

WHETHER YOU'RE a master birder or a casual bird-feeder watcher, National Audubon Society's *Life-List Journal* provides you with a convenient place to record the details of your lifetime species sightings and offers many features to enhance your enjoyment of birds. This attractive book is designed as a practical stay-at-home keepsake that will endure as a permanent chronicle of your treasured experiences with birds. It's the perfect complement to bird identification guides, field notes, and regional checklists.

More than a mere checklist of species, National Audubon Society's *Life-List Journal* allows you to personalize the records of your bird-watching activities. By keeping a chronicle of your bird sightings, you'll preserve the fond memories of your field trips and special sightings and build an archive of your steadily growing knowledge of birds.

ORGANIZATION

The 708 species included in this book are those most commonly seen in the United States (excluding Hawaii) and Canada. They are organized according to their formal classification as set forth in the *American Ornithologists Union's Check-List of American Birds.* This authoritative publication gives common and scientific names, taxonomic status, and geographic ranges of all known species of birds in North America, Central America, Hawaii, and the West Indies.

Species are grouped primarily by order, a taxonomic category that ranks below class and above family. To make the list easier to use, the order *Charadriiformes* (shorebirds) is split into four suborders, and the large order *Passeriformes* (perching birds) is arranged by families and subfamilies.

THE SPECIES ENTRIES

The Latin, or scientific, name is the one given on the right-hand side of each entry. The English, or common, name of each species is on the left-hand side and follows the system used by ornithologists. Shortened names for familiar species can be written with an initial lowercase letter—robin, catbird—but the full name—

American Robin, Gray Catbird—is preferable. When families or groups of birds ("twenty-five species of warblers were seen in the park") are discussed, all the names should be lowercase. When two or more species from the same group ("Blackburnian and Yellow-throated warblers are the prettiest") are named, the "first" name—the name denoting the species—remains capitalized.

LIFE·LIST BASICS

You can use National Audubon Society's *Life-List Journal* to keep a permanent record of your birding observations. You'll find ample space to write the details that are important to you. Among the basics you may wish to note are: date and time; location and habitat; number of birds seen; gender of the birds; behavior of the birds; weather; companions; equipment used; sketches.

The following sample shows how a species entry might look:

Sandhill Crane   {*Grus canadensis*}

DATE *February 14, 2002*   LOCATION *Okefenokee National Wildlife Refuge, Ga. w/ J.J. Audubon*

Aboard rented canoe, using 7 x 35 binoculars; around noon; overcast with some sprinkles. Saw my first ever Sandhill Crane in the Great Prairie near Cooter Lake. Watched a trio for fifteen minutes as they searched for food among the peat beds. Also saw three gators sunning—kept our distance!

ADDITIONAL FEATURES

The illustrated essays and literary excerpts will enhance your knowledge and appreciation of birds. In the back of the journal, the American Birding Association's Principles of Birding Ethics provides pointers on how to observe birds without disturbing wildlife and their habitats. The reference sections list many sources where you can find out more information on birds and birding. The checklist is handy for keeping track of how many birds you've spotted, and it doubles as an index to help you find the species entries quickly.

As you fill this book with your observations and thoughts, remember that maintaining a life list is about more than merely keeping a running count of the birds you've seen: It's about achieving a deeper appreciation of birds and their behaviors and a more intimate understanding of the importance of birds to ecosystems and humanity.

Bird Life List

A Permanent and Personal Record

COMMON NAME	SCIENTIFIC NAME
LOONS	{Order Gaviiformes}

Red-throated Loon
{ *Gavia stellata* }

DATE

LOCATION

Arctic Loon
{ *Gavia arctica* }

DATE

LOCATION

Pacific Loon
{ *Gavia pacifica* }

DATE

LOCATION

Common Loon
{ *Gavia immer* }

DATE

LOCATION

Yellow-billed Loon {*Gavia adamsii*}

DATE   LOCATION

GREBES   {Order Podicipediformes}

Least Grebe {*Tachybaptus dominicus*}

DATE   LOCATION

Pied-billed Grebe {*Podilymbus podiceps*}

DATE   LOCATION

Horned Grebe {*Podiceps auritus*}

DATE   LOCATION

....

Red-necked Grebe   {*Podiceps grisegena*}

DATE   LOCATION

....

Eared Grebe   {*Podiceps nigricollis*}

DATE   LOCATION

....

Western Grebe   {*Aechmophorus occidentalis*}

DATE   LOCATION

....

Clark's Grebe   {*Aechmorphorus clarkii*}

DATE   LOCATION

ALBATROSSES, FULMARS, PETRELS, AND SHEARWATERS   {Order Procellariiformes}

Black-footed Albatross   {*Diomedea nigripes*}

DATE   LOCATION

Laysan Albatross   {*Diomedea immutabilis*}

DATE   LOCATION

Northern Fulmar   {*Fulmarus glacialis*}

DATE   LOCATION

Black-capped Petrel   {*Pterodroma hasitata*}

DATE   LOCATION

Bermuda Petrel

{*Pterodroma cahow*}

DATE

LOCATION

Murphy's Petrel

{*Pterodroma ultima*}

DATE

LOCATION

Cory's Shearwater

{*Calonectris diomedea*}

DATE

LOCATION

Flesh-footed Shearwater

{*Puffinus carneipes*}

DATE

LOCATION

Greater Shearwater {_Puffinus gravis_}

DATE

LOCATION

Wedge-tailed Shearwater {_Puffinus pacificus_}

DATE

LOCATION

Buller's Shearwater {_Puffinus bulleri_}

DATE

LOCATION

Sooty Shearwater {_Puffinus griseus_}

DATE

LOCATION

Short-tailed Shearwater

{*Puffinus tenuirostris*}

DATE   LOCATION

Manx Shearwater

{*Puffinus puffinus*}

DATE   LOCATION

Black-vented Shearwater

{*Puffinus opisthomelas*}

DATE   LOCATION

Townsend's Shearwater

{*Puffinus auricularis*}

DATE   LOCATION

Color

BIRDS APPEAR in a stunning array of shades. Certain species combine colors in striking patterns—the brilliant reds, greens, and blues of the Painted Bunting, for example—to produce some of the most glorious spectacles in the natural world. Other species rival these feathered rainbows with the elegance of a few rich hues, ranging from the bold white of the Great Egret to the deep pink of the Greater Flamingo to the glistening crimson of the Anna's Hummingbird. At the other extreme are species shaded in neutral earth tones, such as the olive-gray Eastern and Western wood-pewees and the brownish Common Snipe.

How do birds get their colors? This question—as basic and pervasive as a child's "Why is the sky blue?"—has intrigued people for centuries. Although early cultures considered bird color to be the result of divine intervention, modern scientists have established that all avian shades, hues, and tints are created by the feather's color-producing properties, which may be pigmentary, structural, or a combination of both. Pigmentary colors result from natural chemical compounds that selectively absorb and reflect the energy of certain wavelengths of light. Structural colors are made by the physical alteration of light on the feather surface.

As a rainbow vividly demonstrates, sunlight is composed of red, orange, yellow, green, blue, indigo, and violet. Each color derives from a particular wavelength of light and becomes apparent as sunlight is split into its constituent wavelengths when it passes through water molecules in the atmosphere. When sunlight strikes a Summer Tanager, for example, the violet-to-green wavelengths are absorbed and the yellow-to-red wavelengths are reflected to produce the characteristic brilliant reds of the bird. Black is the result when the energy of all wavelengths of light is absorbed, as in the Common Raven; white occurs when the energy of all wavelengths is reflected, as in the Snowy Owl.

Anna's Hummingbird is crowned with a cap of glistening crimson.

PIGMENTARY COLORS

Pigmentary colors come from granules of pigment deposited in the feather microstructure. There are three major groups of feather pigments: melanins, carotenoids, and porphyrins. Melanins, found almost universally throughout the animal kingdom (except in albinos), are responsible for earth tones such as the black of the Black-backed Woodpecker, the brown of the Golden Eagle, and the gray of the Red-throated Loon. Birds have cells in their skin called melanoplasts that synthesize melanins from the amino acid tyrosine. Melanoplasts are mobile and deposit the melanin granules into the cells that become the barbs and barbules (the tiny hooks that hold the barbs of the feather together) of bird feathers. Different concentrations of melanins deposited throughout the plumage create the variety of colors and such patterns as barring and speckling. Melanins are also important because they make feathers more resistant to fraying and abrasion, and they aid in thermoregulation by absorbing radiant energy.

Carotenoid pigments make bright reds, yellows, and oranges. Unlike melanins, carotenoids are not synthesized but obtained directly from the bird's diet. The pink plumage of the Greater Flamingo, for example, is due to a pigment that comes directly from the food that it filters from the water (tiny crustaceans, insects, and algae), and the bright red feathers of the male House Finch result from eating carotenoid-rich seeds. Carotenoids are stored in egg yolks and body fats, and accumulate in the lipids contained within growing feather cells. As feathers mature, carotenoids are deposited in the barbs and barbules.

Porphyrin pigments are responsible for the reddish-brown feathers found in a number of bird orders, including owls, and for the bright green colors of a few species, such as the Wattled Jacana. Porphyrins are chemically related to hemoglobin and liver bile pigments that contain iron, but the best-understood porphyrin pigment in birds contains copper. Because they are chemically unstable and degrade in sunlight, porphyrins are usually found only in new feathers.

STRUCTURAL COLORS

The scattering of light by minute melanin particles near the feather surface is responsible for the brilliant blues of the Lazuli Bunting, the bright greens of the Military Macaw, and the iridescence of the Common Grackle. In general, short (blue and violet) wavelengths of light are scattered, while long (red and yellow) wavelengths are absorbed. The wavelength of light scattered depends upon the size of the particle doing the scattering: For example, green structural colors are pro-

Clockwise from upper left: Summer Tanager; Great Egret; Greater Flamingo; Snowy Owl; Painted Bunting; Mallard drake; Scarlet Macaw; House Finch; Peacock

duced by larger particles than are blue structural colors.

In some species, pigmentary and structural colors work together. Wild Budgerigars are green because a structural blue acts in concert with a carotenoid-based yellow pigment filter and a layer of melanin pigment. Domestic Budgerigars appear in a variety of colors because they have been selectively bred to block the deposition of certain pigments.

As a drake Wood Duck glides across a pond, it appears as if its feathers are changing from metallic green to purple to black. Iridescent colors, such as those found in ducks, peacocks, and hummingbirds, are caused by the interference of light waves as they reflect from the inner and outer surfaces of feather structures. The structures may be granules or tubules of melanin, or layers of keratin (proteins making up the epidermal tissues). Wavelengths of light reflected from the inner surfaces become out of phase with equivalent wavelengths of light reflected from the outer surfaces, due to differences in the distance traveled to each surface.

The iridescent Wood Duck drake

The wavelengths reflected from the inner and outer surfaces interfere with each other, leaving only the complementary wavelengths. When the viewing angle is varied, the distance light travels to the inner and outer surfaces alters, as does the color produced.

The Meaning of Color

While scientists have successfully explained the *how* of bird color, many questions remain concerning the *why*. Since Darwin postulated his theory of sexual selection in 1871, scientists have made important discoveries about the evolutionary significance of color. Plumage color and patterning provide camouflage in the American Bittern, identify individual birds in Ruddy Turnstones, signal dominance in House Sparrows, and may convey competitive status in Lazuli Buntings. Moreover, recent evidence supports the theory that females assess a male's quality by his color—the basic logic being that ornamental traits are energetically and physiologically costly to produce and maintain, and increase the bird's risk of being noticed by predators. The males that best endure these costs signal their underlying quality. By choosing to mate with them, females are reasonably assured that their offspring will gain genes that are resistant to disease and parasites.

Audubon's Shearwater   {*Puffinus lherminieri*}

DATE   LOCATION

Wilson's Storm-Petrel   {*Oceanites oceanicus*}

DATE   LOCATION

Fork-tailed Storm-Petrel   {*Oceanodroma furcata*}

DATE   LOCATION

Leach's Storm-Petrel   {*Oceanodroma leucorhoa*}

DATE   LOCATION

Ashy Storm-Petrel   {*Oceanodroma homochroa*}

DATE   LOCATION

Band-rumped Storm-Petrel   {*Oceanodroma castro*}

DATE   LOCATION

Black Storm-Petrel   {*Oceanodroma melania*}

DATE   LOCATION

TROPICBIRDS, BOOBIES, GANNETS, PELICANS,
CORMORANTS, ANHINGAS, AND FRIGATEBIRDS   {Order Pelecaniformes}

White-tailed Tropicbird   {*Phaethon lepturus*}

DATE   LOCATION

Red-billed Tropicbird   {*Phaethon aethereus*}

DATE   LOCATION

Masked Booby   {*Sula dactylatra*}

DATE   LOCATION

Blue-footed Booby   {*Sula nebouxii*}

DATE   LOCATION

Brown Booby   {*Sula leucogaster*}

DATE   LOCATION

Red-footed Booby   {*Sula sula*}

DATE   LOCATION

Northern Gannet   {*Morus bassanus*}

DATE *Summer 1957*   LOCATION *Gaspé, Que. Canada*

American White Pelican   {*Pelecanus erythrorhynchos*}

DATE   LOCATION

Brown Pelican   {*Pelecanus occidentalis*}

DATE   LOCATION

I am like a pelican of the wilderness: I am like an owl of the desert. I watch, and am as a sparrow alone upon the house top.

(Psalm 102:6—7)

Great Cormorant

DATE

{ Phalacrocorax carbo }

LOCATION

Double-crested Cormorant

DATE 4-16-03

{ Phalacrocorax auritus }

LOCATION Muscatatuc & NWR, Jackson Co, IN (25 cen)
may not be first sighting

Neotropic Cormorant

DATE

{ Phalacrocorax brasilianus }

LOCATION

Brandt's Cormorant

DATE

{ Phalacrocorax penicillatus }

LOCATION

TROPICBIRDS, BOOBIES, GANNETS, PELICANS,
CORMORANTS, ANHINGAS, AND FRIGATEBIRDS *(cont'd)*   {Order Pelecaniformes}

Pelagic Cormorant   {*Phalacrocorax pelagicus*}

DATE   LOCATION

Red-faced Cormorant   {*Phalacrocorax urile*}

DATE   LOCATION

Anhinga   {*Anhinga anhinga*}

DATE   LOCATION

Magnificent Frigatebird   {*Fregata magnificens*}

DATE   LOCATION

American Bittern   {*Botaurus lentiginosus*}

DATE   LOCATION

Least Bittern   {*Ixobrychus exilis*}

DATE   LOCATION

Great Blue Heron   {*Ardea herodias*}

DATE   LOCATION

Great Egret   {*Ardea alba*}

DATE   LOCATION

HERONS, IBISES AND SPOONBILLS, AND STORKS *(cont'd)*   {Order Ciconiiformes}

Snowy Egret   {*Egretta thula*}

DATE   LOCATION

Little Blue Heron   {*Egretta caerulea*}

DATE   LOCATION

Tricolored Heron   {*Egretta tricolor*}

DATE   LOCATION

Reddish Egret   {*Egretta rufescens*}

DATE   LOCATION

Cattle Egret

{*Bubulcus ibis*}

DATE

LOCATION

Green Heron

{*Butorides virescens*}

DATE

LOCATION

Black-crowned Night-Heron

{*Nycticorax nycticorax*}

DATE

LOCATION

Yellow-crowned Night-Heron

{*Nyctanassa violacea*}

DATE

LOCATION

HERONS, IBISES AND SPOONBILLS, AND STORKS *(cont'd)*   {Order Ciconiiformes}

....

White Ibis   {*Eudocimus albus*}

DATE   LOCATION

....

Glossy Ibis   {*Plegadis falcinellus*}

DATE   LOCATION

....

White-faced Ibis   {*Plegadis chihi*}

DATE   LOCATION

....

Roseate Spoonbill   {*Ajaia ajaja*}

DATE   LOCATION

Wood Stork {*Mycteria americana*}

DATE   LOCATION

FLAMINGOS {Order Phoenicopteriformes}

Greater Flamingo {*Phoenicopterus ruber*}

DATE   LOCATION

SWANS, GEESE, AND DUCKS {Order Anseriformes}

Fulvous Whistling-Duck {*Dendrocygna bicolor*}

DATE   LOCATION

Black-bellied Whistling-Duck {*Dendrocygna autumnalis*}

DATE   LOCATION

Tundra Swan   {Cygnus columbianus}

DATE   LOCATION

Trumpeter Swan   {Cygnus buccinator}

DATE Jul   02   LOCATION S.E. Kalamazoo CO, MI

Mute Swan   {Cygnus olor}

DATE   LOCATION

Greater White-fronted Goose   {Anser albifrons}

DATE   LOCATION

Snow Goose
{ *Chen caerulescens* }

DATE   LOCATION

*Behold the fowls of the air: for
they sow not, neither do they reap,
nor gather into barns, yet your
heavenly Father feedeth them. Are
ye not much better than they?*

(Matthew 6:26)

Ross's Goose
{ *Chen rossii* }

DATE   LOCATION

Emperor Goose
{ *Chen canagica* }

DATE   LOCATION

Brant
{ *Branta bernicla* }

DATE   LOCATION

SWANS, GEESE, AND DUCKS *(cont'd)*   {Order Anseriformes}

Canada Goose   {*Branta canadensis*}

DATE

LOCATION

Wood Duck   {*Aix sponsa*}

DATE 4-3-03

4-16-03 (2 sight) pairs sighted
@ Muse-NWR

LOCATION Muscatatuck NWR, Jackson Co. IN
also River otter

Green-winged Teal   {*Anas crecca*}

DATE

LOCATION

American Black Duck   {*Anas rubripes*}

DATE

LOCATION

Mottled Duck {*Anas fulvigula*}

DATE

LOCATION

Mallard {*Anas platyrhynchos*}

DATE *Various*

LOCATION Nobl PSUP/4, IN
Goshen, IN, other pond locations
Northern & Central IN

Northern Pintail {*Anas acuta*}

DATE

LOCATION

Garganey {*Anas querquedula*}

DATE

LOCATION

Blue-winged Teal   {*Anas discors*}

DATE 9-5-83   LOCATION Muscatatuck NWR Jackson Co, IN
4-16-03 Muscatatuck NWR

Cinnamon Teal   {*Anas cyanoptera*}

DATE   LOCATION

Northern Shoveler   {*Anas clypeata*}

DATE 9-5-03   LOCATION Muscatatuck NWR Jackson Co, IN
4-16-03 Muscatatuck NWP   (Not first)

Gadwall   {*Anas strepera*}

DATE   LOCATION

Courtship

COURTSHIP BREAKS down the barriers of territorial distance that keep most birds apart. Males attract mates with elaborate behaviors and intricate songs, females choose their ideal partner, and each species has its own unique set of rituals. Exactly how birds make their courtship choices is little understood, but clearly the stakes are high for both sexes and for the species as a whole.

ATTRACTING A MATE

For species in which the two sexes look alike, such as waxwings, jays, and sparrows, the first instinct of a territorial male is to chase away intruding members, regardless of gender. The most subtle of behaviors help defending males to recognize members of the opposite sex: Female songbirds, on approaching a territory, usually act submissive, holding their wings slightly open and their head at a downward angle. Such behaviors relax the aggressive male. In other species, the male's extraordinary plumage exists to attract mates—the peacock being the most popular example of this phenomenon. In arctic climates, where the nesting season is brief,

The Hummingbirds and Two Varieties of Orchids (1882–1884), *by Martin Johnson Heade*

gender roles are sometimes reversed. Female phalaropes, for example, wear the bright colors usually associated with males, and use them to attract a succession of dull-plumaged mates. The female leaves each father to incubate and tend a clutch of eggs, allowing her to produce several clutches in the fleeting arctic summer.

COURTSHIP RITUALS AND GIFTS

Behavioral displays coupled with arresting sounds also draw attention: Male frigatebirds inflate their scarlet throat pouches to the size of beach balls and indulge in an all-body quiver, trembling their extended wings while emitting odd rattling noises. When a dozen males gather, all of them inflating, quivering, and rattling, females rely on subtle differences in the performances to choose among competing suitors. Similar group displays drive mate selection in a range of birds, including prairie-chickens, manakins, and certain hummingbirds. In these species, groups of males return each year to a traditional courtship location, known as a lek. To attract mates, the males perform stylized dances accompanied by their own ancient music of whoops, buzzes, clicks, and snaps. The male woodcock engages in extraordinary acrobatics, flying three hundred feet high in a spiraling pattern, then tumbling to the ground like a falling leaf. The upward flight is accented by the whistling sound of wind passing through his wing tips, and the descent is punctuated by excited squeaks. The performance ends with a mechanical *peent* as the hopeful male waits for a female to fly into his courting arena. If successful, the male mates with the attracted female, who has the sole responsibility for incubation and protection of chicks. Woodcocks continue to dance through the spring, hoping to attract additional partners. Males fit enough to repeatedly perform this rigorous courtship flight may be seen by females as sturdy stock to father offspring.

Courtship also often involves food offerings. Receptive females quiver their wings, much like begging chicks, then accept the food. The male's offerings may indicate his skill at feeding—a prowess essential for successful chick-rearing. The male tern dangles food, typically herring or hake, in front of a prospective mate, then takes flight with the ceremonial fish flashing from its beak, enticing the female to fly in tandem. For fruit-eating birds such as waxwings and cardinals, the courtship prize presented by the male is a juicy berry.

Waterbirds often use nesting material as courtship offerings. Male cormorants, spoonbills, and herons such as the Great Blue Heron offer sticks and twigs to attract a mate, while male Adélie Penguins present a small rock as a token of their intentions. Acceptance of the nesting material confirms that the male has

Great Blue Herons offer sticks and twigs to entice a mate.

successfully approached a member of the opposite sex, and that she shares his interest in mating.

PAIR FORMATION

Engagement periods, during which individuals frequent the nesting territory months before breeding, occur among many nonmigratory species, such as Wrentits and Eastern Bluebirds. Albatross and puffins maintain even longer engagements, sometimes pairing a year before the first egg is laid. Because of food limitations, migratory birds such as warblers and egrets usually do not visit nesting sites early.

After pair formation, birds learn to recognize their mates by appearance, sound, or, in some cases, location of the breeding site. Many birds are faithful to the same mate year after year. This is especially true for long-lived birds such as puffins, albatross, and swans. An Atlantic Puffin may keep the same mate and reside in the same burrow for fifteen or more consecutive years. Some Mute Swans are known to have stayed together as a pair for as long as eight years. When one member of the pair died, the "bereaved" did not mate again for three years. Faithfulness to a mate is also common among many familiar backyard birds, such as American Robins and Northern Mockingbirds. But such loyal monogamy is not always the case: A detailed study of Song Sparrows showed that among two hundred pairs, only eight pairs retained the same mate from one year to the next. Regardless, a common pattern exists: Females select the males they will have as their mates.

Rufous-naped Lark display-dancing (top); Magnificent Frigatebird male in courtship display (center); Tufted Puffin pair (bottom)

Eurasian Wigeon {*Anas penelope*}

DATE

LOCATION

American Wigeon {*Anas americana*}

DATE

LOCATION

Canvasback {*Aythya valisineria*}

DATE Late 50's early 60's

LOCATION Goshen IN - Elkhart River Dam

Redhead {*Aythya americana*}

DATE

LOCATION

Ring-necked Duck　　　　{*Aythya collaris*}

DATE　　　　　　　　　　　　　　　　LOCATION

Tufted Duck　　　　{*Aythya fuligula*}

DATE　　　　　　　　　　　　　　　　LOCATION

Greater Scaup　　　　{*Aythya marila*}

DATE　　　　　　　　　　　　　　　　LOCATION

Lesser Scaup　　　　{*Aythya affinis*}

DATE　　　　　　　　　　　　　　　　LOCATION

Common Eider

{ Somateria mollissima }

DATE

LOCATION

King Eider

{ Somateria spectabilis }

DATE

LOCATION

Spectacled Eider

{ Somateria fischeri }

DATE

LOCATION

Steller's Eider

{ Polysticta stelleri }

DATE

LOCATION

Harlequin Duck

{*Histrionicus histrionicus*}

DATE

LOCATION

Oldsquaw

{*Clangula hyemalis*}

DATE

LOCATION

Black Scoter

{*Melanitta nigra*}

DATE

LOCATION

Surf Scoter

{*Melanitta perspicillata*}

DATE

LOCATION

White-winged Scoter

{ *Melanitta fusca* }

DATE   LOCATION

Common Goldeneye

{ *Bucephala clangula* }

DATE   LOCATION

Barrow's Goldeneye

{ *Bucephala islandica* }

DATE   LOCATION

Bufflehead

{ *Bucephala albeola* }

DATE   LOCATION

Hooded Merganser   {*Lophodytes cucullatus*}

DATE   LOCATION

Common Merganser   {*Mergus merganser*}

DATE   LOCATION

Red-breasted Merganser   {*Mergus serrator*}

DATE   LOCATION

Ruddy Duck   {*Oxyura jamaicensis*}

DATE   LOCATION

Masked Duck {*Oxyura dominica*}

DATE   LOCATION

Black Vulture {*Coragyps atratus*}

DATE   LOCATION

Turkey Vulture {*Cathartes aura*}

DATE 3-5-03   LOCATION Muscatatuck NWR Jackson Co, IN
                                       (Not First)

California Condor {*Gymnogyps californianus*}

DATE   LOCATION

Osprey

{*Pandion haliaetus*}

DATE unknown- first sighting
(early 1980's ?)
4-16-2003

LOCATION Morse Dam, Noblesville, IN
Muscatuck NWR, Jackson Co, IN

Hook-billed Kite

{*Chondrohierax uncinatus*}

DATE

LOCATION

Swallow-tailed Kite

{*Elanoides forficatus*}

DATE

LOCATION

White-tailed Kite

{*Elanus leucurus*}

DATE

LOCATION

Snail Kite

{ *Rostrhamus sociabilis* }

DATE _Summer 2002 (?)_

LOCATION _Wayne Co, IN N.W. of Greens Fork and North of SR 38 (possible stray)_

Mississippi Kite

{ *Ictinia mississippiensis* }

DATE

LOCATION

Bald Eagle

{ *Haliaeetus leucocephalus* }

DATE
Oct, 2007
Oct, 1998 (First
_4-16-03_

LOCATION
Northern MN - 8 spotted on trip
Rolling Ridge, Shenandoah R, W.V
Muscatatuck NWR, Jackson Co, IN

Northern Harrier

{ *Circus cyaneus* }

DATE

LOCATION

Sharp-shinned Hawk   {*Accipiter striatus*}

DATE   LOCATION

Cooper's Hawk   {*Accipiter cooperii*}

DATE   LOCATION

Nov   2002   Noblesville, River Trail, IN
Mar 30, 2003 (?)   "   "   "   IN

Northern Goshawk   {*Accipiter gentilis*}

DATE   LOCATION

Common Black-Hawk   {*Buteogallus anthracinus*}

DATE   LOCATION

Harris's Hawk {*Parabuteo unicinctus*}

DATE

LOCATION

Gray Hawk {*Buteo nitidus*}

DATE

LOCATION

Red-shouldered Hawk {*Buteo lineatus*}

DATE
Nov.   2012

LOCATION
Appalichicola   Forest, FL

Broad-winged Hawk {*Buteo platypterus*}

DATE

LOCATION

Short-tailed Hawk   {*Buteo brachyurus*}

DATE   LOCATION

Swainson's Hawk   {*Buteo swainsoni*}

DATE   LOCATION

White-tailed Hawk   {*Buteo albicaudatus*}

DATE   LOCATION

Zone-tailed Hawk   {*Buteo albonotatus*}

DATE   LOCATION

Red-tailed Hawk

{ *Buteo jamaicensis* }

DATE un known - frtquent sightings

LOCATION Noblesville, IN
OH, IL, WI

Ferruginous Hawk

{ *Buteo regalis* }

DATE

LOCATION

Rough-legged Hawk

{ *Buteo lagopus* }

DATE

LOCATION

Golden Eagle

{ *Aquila chrysaetos* }

DATE

LOCATION

Crested Caracara   {Caracara plancus}

DATE   LOCATION

American Kestrel   {Falco sparverius}

DATE *frequent*   LOCATION *Noblesville twp, Hamilton Co, IN*

Merlin   {Falco columbarius}

DATE   LOCATION

Aplomado Falcon   {Falco femoralis}

DATE   LOCATION

Peregrine Falcon   {*Falco peregrinus*}

DATE   LOCATION

Gyrfalcon   {*Falco rusticolus*}

DATE   LOCATION

Prairie Falcon   {*Falco mexicanus*}

DATE   LOCATION

PHEASANTS, GROUSE, AND QUAILS   {Order Galliformes}

Gray Partridge   {*Perdix perdix*}

DATE   LOCATION

Chukar   {*Alectoris chukar*}

DATE   LOCATION

Ring-necked Pheasant   {*Phasianus colchicus*}

DATE occassional   LOCATION Elkhart, Lagrange Cos, IN

Spruce Grouse   {*Dendragapus canadensis*}

DATE   LOCATION

Blue Grouse   {*Dendragapus obscurus*}

DATE   LOCATION

Bowerbirds, such as the Satin Bowerbird of Australia, are known as the "Picassos of the bird world" because of their artistically arched nests.

Nests

USING THEIR natural assets—beaks and feet—birds are able to craft durable nests that are resistant to climatic extremes and practically predator-proof. Twigs, leaves, grass, and feathers provide structure and insulation, and some birds customize their homes with stones, mud, and saliva. There are nests so small that they're covered by the belly of a sitting bird, and there are nests so large that the parents disappear inside to incubate. Nests can be built from scratch, excavated, or adapted from those already in existence. Although nests vary greatly in form and complexity, the function of every nest is essentially the same: to serve as a cradle in which birds lay their eggs and incubate them until they hatch.

CRAFTING A HOME

The craftsmanship inherent in nests exemplifies the degree of artistry to be found in the natural world. Many birds exhibit an amazing aptitude for architecture. It's amazing what useful, intricate, even lovely nests birds can construct without specialized tools. Carvers—typified by woodpeckers, who have strong, pointed bills and heads that can withstand sharp percussions—chisel deep, smooth-walled chambers with rounded doorways out of solid wood. Miners, including kingfishers, motmots, and jacamars,

Meadowlarks *by John James Audubon*

American Oystercatcher

dig shafts into banks of clay, loam, or sand. Potters—cliff swallows or house martins, for example—make their nests out of mud or clay. Basket makers, such as the spinetails of Central America, interlace twigs or leaves. Felt makers, such as hummingbirds and bushtits, press downy materials into a compact fabric. Weavers, notably the weaverbirds of Africa and the Black-cowled Oriole of Central America, lace fibers through their nest fabric from side to side, often tying simple knots.

Whether elaborate or simple in appearance, every nest is designed to support the weight of the chicks to be reared. Cassin's Malimbe, which lives in central Africa, weaves a two-foot-long vertical tube around the nest entrance to foil intruders. The Blue-footed Booby, nesting on the Galápagos Islands, incubates its eggs in a crude scrape on the bare ground.

MOUND BUILDERS

Sometimes referred to as thermometer birds, mound builders rely on heat from the sun or surrounding environment to incubate their eggs. Their nests range from a simple pit dug in the sand to an immense heap of leaf litter and soil as wide as thirty-five feet in diameter. The Mallee Fowl, which inhabits the dry, open country of inland southwestern Australia, and the Scrub-fowl, which is widespread from the Philippines across to New Guinea, Australia, and western Pacific Islands, both bury their eggs in a mound, where they are incubated by the heat generated by the sun and the decaying vegetable matter. Australia's dark, jungle-dwelling Brush-turkey spends three to six weeks constructing its mound, which can contain up to fifty-eight eggs. The Dusky Megapode, which lives on many of the islands of Indonesia, builds its mound at altitudes as high as six hundred meters, as well as on the edge of beaches.

Coot with chicks

NO-NESTERS

Whether or not they have an enclosed nest in which to put them, the majority of bird parents incubate their eggs. Whip-poor-wills deposit their eggs on the ground among leaf litter, usually in dense woods. Nighthawks lay their two eggs on top of a flat rock on a hillside or in open woods— some, in response to urbanization, deposit their eggs on gravel rooftops. The lack of a nest reduces the odds that a hungry predator will spot the eggs. Several bird species now place their nests in urban settings. Least Terns and killdeers routinely nest on rooftops, where they withstand surface temperatures of up to 140° Fahrenheit.

Gannets

The Fairy Tern, a small, white-plumed species that ranges throughout sheltered coasts and islands of southern and western Australia, New Zealand, and New Caledonia, chooses the most precarious of sites for its nest. Even if stunted plants, clumps of *Arctotheca populifolia,* or raised shell mounds are accessible, the female deposits her single egg in some little depression on a branch that may not be more than an inch in diameter. She then rests in front of the egg, holding it in position with the feathers of her breast. In lieu of a tree, the Fairy Tern selects a ledge of rock on which it would seem almost impossible for the egg to remain in place. The young terns, once hatched, have strong toes. From the moment of birth, they cling with a tenacious grip to their insecure perches. Even more peculiar are the Emperor and King penguins of the southern oceans, who balance their single egg on top of their feet, and shield it from the cold Antarctic ice under a fold of warm belly skin.

Cavity Nesters

Eared Grebe

The shelter and safety provided by cavities appeal to many bird species, including woodpeckers, parrots, trogons, kingfishers, and starlings. Some use natural cavities as they find them, others tailor the space to their particular needs. The female Red-billed Hornbill of Africa provides safety for her eggs by first entering a tree cavity and then plastering herself inside—walling up the entrance with mud and saliva, leaving a slit just narrow enough to put her beak out to accept food from the male. She endures this self-imposed exile for the entire incubation period, which lasts four to six weeks. In North America, duck species such as the Black-bellied Whistling-Duck and Common

Merganser nest in tree cavities. The optimum natural cavities for Wood Ducks are in trees twenty feet above the ground. Ferruginous Owls nest in abandoned woodpecker holes in mesquite, cottonwoods, and saguaro cacti. Chestnut-backed Chickadees also nest in abandoned woodpecker holes, or in cavities they excavate themselves, usually in pine, oak, and douglas-fir snags.

AN ASSORTMENT OF NESTS

The Osprey, a large, fish-eating raptor, builds remarkable stick nests almost one yard wide and two yards deep in treetops or on platforms. The birds use the same nest year after year, adding material until it becomes an enormous mass six to eight feet in diameter. Often the nest is built up to the point that it breaks down the tree in which it was made. At the opposite end of the avian spectrum, hummingbirds form felted cups of plant downs and soft fibers, bind them together with spider webbing, and ornament them with bits of moss and lichen so that they closely resemble the limb on which they are saddled, creating the smallest and most perfectly camouflaged nests.

An Osprey constructs its elaborate nest.

Male weaverbirds in Africa sling their dense and durable nests from the tips of slender twigs high in the trees. The aerial isolation helps protect them. As their name implies, weaverbirds ingeniously twist their nesting threads into loops and hitches that hold to perfection. The nest is woven to hang like a sac, attached to the tree branches by its edges. Or it is turned into a covered basket with a side opening and dangles from a strand of fibers. A long, tubelike entrance helps to foil any avian predator that might alight on the nest and try to claw inside with its feet. The nests are in plain sight, but even the most agile snake has difficulty reaching them.

The Ovenbird, a species of wood warbler native to North America, builds its home on the ground, constructing a nest of grasses and leaf skeletons, arching the top over with roots or leaves and leaving a small, side entrance somewhat suggestive of an old-fashioned oven. Situated in wooded land, the nest is inconspicuous and well concealed.

The cavity-dwelling Rose-ringed Parakeet

Willow Ptarmigan   {*Lagopus lagopus*}

DATE   LOCATION

Rock Ptarmigan   {*Lagopus mutus*}

DATE   LOCATION

White-tailed Ptarmigan   {*Lagopus leucurus*}

DATE   LOCATION

Ruffed Grouse   {*Bonasa umbellus*}

DATE   LOCATION

Sage Grouse {*Centrocercus urophasianus*}

DATE

LOCATION

Greater Prairie-chicken {*Tympanuchus cupido*}

DATE

LOCATION

Lesser Prairie-chicken {*Tympanuchus pallidicinctus*}

DATE

LOCATION

Sharp-tailed Grouse {*Tympanuchus phasianellus*}

DATE

LOCATION

Wild Turkey

DATE

{ *Meleagris gallopavo* }

LOCATION

Montezuma Quail

DATE

{ *Cyrtonyx montezumae* }

LOCATION

Northern Bobwhite

DATE

{ *Colinus virginianus* }

LOCATION

Scaled Quail

DATE

{ *Callipepla squamata* }

LOCATION

ODE TO A NIGHTINGALE

"ODE TO A NIGHTINGALE" was written in May 1819. Afflicted with tuberculosis, John Keats was convalescing in Hempstead, England, under the guidance of his friend Charles Brown, who wrote the following account of the making of the poem: "In the spring of 1819 a nightingale had built her nest near my house, Keats felt a tranquil and continual joy in her song; and one morning he took his chair from the breakfast-table to the grass-plot under a plum-tree, where he sat for two or three hours. When he came into the house, I perceived he had some scraps of paper in his hand, and these he was quietly thrusting behind the books. On inquiry, I found those scraps, four or five in number, contained his poetic feeling on the song of our nightingale."

1.

My heart aches, and a drowsy numbness pains
　　My sense, as though of hemlock I had drunk,
Or emptied some dull opiate to the drains
　　One minute past, and Lethe-wards had sunk:
'Tis not through envy of thy happy lot,
　　But being too happy in thine happiness,—
　　　　That thou, light-winged Dryad of the trees,
　　　　　　In some melodious plot
　　Of beechen green, and shadows numberless,
　　　　Singest of summer in full-throated ease.

2.

O, for a draught of vintage! that hath been
　　Cool'd a long age in the deep-delved earth,
Tasting of Flora and the country green,
　　Dance, and Provençal song, and sunburnt mirth!
O for a beaker full of the warm South,
　　Full of the true, the blushful Hippocrene,
　　　　With beaded bubbles winking at the brim,
　　　　　　And purple-stained mouth;
　　That I might drink, and leave the world unseen,
　　　　And with thee fade away into the forest dim:

3.

Fade far away, dissolve, and quite forget
　　What thou among the leaves hast never known,
The weariness, the fever, and the fret
　　Here, where men sit and hear each other groan;
Where palsy shakes a few, sad, last gray hairs,
　　Where youth grows pale, and spectre-thin, and dies;
　　　　Where but to think is to be full of sorrow
　　　　　　And leaden-eyed despairs,
　　Where Beauty cannot keep her lustrous eyes,
　　　　Or new Love pine at them beyond to-morrow.

4.

Away! away! for I will fly to thee,
　　Not charioted by Bacchus and his pards,
But on the viewless wings of Poesy,
　　Though the dull brain perplexes and retards:
Already with thee! tender is the night,
　　And haply the Queen-Moon is on her throne,
　　　　Cluster'd around by all her starry Fays;
　　　　　　But here there is no light,
　　Save what from heaven is with the breezes blown
　　　　Through verdurous glooms and winding mossy ways.

5.

I cannot see what flowers are at my feet,
    Nor what soft incense hangs upon the boughs,
But, in embalmed darkness, guess each sweet
    Wherewith the seasonable month endows
The grass, the thicket, and the fruit-tree wild;
    White hawthorn, and the pastoral eglantine;
      Fast fading violets cover'd up in leaves;
        And mid-May's eldest child,
    The coming musk-rose, full of dewy wine,
      The murmurous haunt of flies on summer eves.

6.

Darkling I listen; and, for many a time
    I have been half in love with easeful Death,
Call'd him soft names in many a mused rhyme,
    To take into the air my quiet breath;
Now more than ever seems it rich to die,
    To cease upon the midnight with no pain,
      While thou art pouring forth thy soul abroad
        In such an ecstasy!
    Still wouldst thou sing, and I have ears in vain—
      To thy high requiem become a sod.

7.

Thou wast not born for death, immortal Bird!
    No hungry generations tread thee down;
The voice I hear this passing night was heard
    In ancient days by emperor and clown:
Perhaps the self-same song that found a path
    Through the sad heart of Ruth, when, sick for home,
      She stood in tears amid the alien corn;
        The same that oft-times hath
    Charm'd magic casements, opening on the foam
      Of perilous seas, in faery lands forlorn.

8.

Forlorn! the very word is like a bell
    To toil me back from thee to my sole self!
Adieu! the fancy cannot cheat so well
    As she is fam'd to do, deceiving elf.
Adieu! adieu! thy plaintive anthem fades
    Past the near meadows, over the still stream
      Up the hill-side; and now 'tis buried deep
        In the next valley-glades:
    Was it a vision, or a waking dream?
      Fled is that music:—Do I wake or sleep?

JOHN KEATS

PHEASANTS, GROUSE, AND QUAILS *(cont'd)*   {Order Galliformes}

Gambel's Quail   {*Callipepla gambelii*}

DATE   LOCATION

California Quail   {*Callipepla californica*}

DATE   LOCATION

Mountain Quail   {*Oreortyx pictus*}

DATE   LOCATION

RAILS, COOTS, LIMPKINS, AND CRANES   {Order Gruiformes}

Yellow Rail   {*Coturnicops noveboracensis*}

DATE   LOCATION

Black Rail

DATE

{*Laterallus jamaicensis*}

LOCATION

Clapper Rail

DATE

{*Rallus longirostris*}

LOCATION

King Rail

DATE

{*Rallus elegans*}

LOCATION

Virginia Rail

DATE

{*Rallus limicola*}

LOCATION

Sora   {*Porzana carolina*}

DATE   LOCATION

Purple Gallinule   {*Porphyrula martinica*}

DATE   LOCATION

Common Moorhen   {*Gallinula chloropus*}

DATE   LOCATION

American Coot   {*Fulica americana*}

DATE   LOCATION

Limpkin
{ *Aramus guarauna* }

DATE

LOCATION

Sandhill Crane
{ *Grus canadensis* }

DATE

LOCATION

Whooping Crane
{ *Grus americana* }

DATE

LOCATION

SHOREBIRDS, WADERS, GULLS, AND DIVING BIRDS
Plovers, Oystercatchers, Stilts, and Avocets

{ Order Charadriiformes }
{ Suborder Charadrii }

Northern Lapwing
{ *Vanellus vanellus* }

DATE

LOCATION

Plovers, Oystercatchers, Stilts, and Avocets (cont'd)   {Suborder Charadrii}

Black-bellied Plover   {*Pluvialis squatarola*}

DATE   LOCATION

American Golden-Plover   {*Pluvialis dominicus*}

DATE   LOCATION

Pacific Golden-Plover   {*Pluvialis fulva*}

DATE   LOCATION

Snowy Plover   {*Charadrius alexandrinus*}

DATE   LOCATION

Wilson's Plover

DATE

{*Charadrius wilsonia*}

LOCATION

Semipalmated Plover

DATE

{*Charadrius semipalmatus*}

LOCATION

Piping Plover

DATE

{*Charadrius melodus*}

LOCATION

Killdeer

DATE

{*Charadrius vociferus*}

LOCATION

Mountain Plover   {*Charadrius montanus*}

DATE   LOCATION

American Oystercatcher   {*Haematopus palliatus*}

DATE   LOCATION

Black Oystercatcher   {*Haematopus bachmani*}

DATE   LOCATION

Black-necked Stilt   {*Himantopus mexicanus*}

DATE   LOCATION

American Avocet　　　　　　　　　{ *Recurvirostra americana* }

DATE　　　　　　　　　　　　　　　LOCATION

Jacanas and Sandpipers　　　　　　{ Suborder Scolopaci }

Northern Jacana　　　　　　　　　{ *Jacana spinosa* }

DATE　　　　　　　　　　　　　　　LOCATION

Greater Yellowlegs　　　　　　　　{ *Tringa melanoleuca* }

DATE　　　　　　　　　　　　　　　LOCATION

Lesser Yellowlegs　　　　　　　　　{ *Tringa flavipes* }

DATE　　　　　　　　　　　　　　　LOCATION

Solitary Sandpiper   {*Tringa solitaria*}

DATE   LOCATION

Willet   {*Catoptrophorus semipalmatus*}

DATE   LOCATION

Wandering Tattler   {*Heteroscelus incanus*}

DATE   LOCATION

Gray-tailed Tattler   {*Heteroscelus brevipes*}

DATE   LOCATION

Spotted Sandpiper   { *Actitis macularia* }

DATE   LOCATION

Upland Sandpiper   { *Bartramia longicauda* }

DATE   LOCATION

Whimbrel   { *Numenius phaeopus* }

DATE   LOCATION

Bristle-thighed Curlew   { *Numenius tahitiensis* }

DATE   LOCATION

Long-billed Curlew   {Numenius americanus}

DATE   LOCATION

Black-tailed Godwit   {Limosa limosa}

DATE   LOCATION

Hudsonian Godwit   {Limosa haemastica}

DATE   LOCATION

Bar-tailed Godwit   {Limosa lapponica}

DATE   LOCATION

Eggs

B I R D S   I N H E R I T E D   their egg-laying habit from their reptilian ancestors, most of which deposited their white, leathery-skinned eggs in casually built nests. While nearly all mammals evolved long ago from tending external eggs, birds remain bound to the necessity of laying and caring for their precious clutches.

ADAPTATIONS

Birds are conservative egg layers compared to most fish and insects: While, for example, female cod may produce up to ten million eggs and abandon them to the mercy of the sea, birds lay just a few eggs, sometimes only one every other year, and go to great lengths to preserve them. The number of eggs that they lay, the length of incubation, the color, size, and even shape are determined by the demands of specific habitats.

Egg color is strongly influenced by nest location. Woodpeckers, Tree Swallows, Purple Martins, and other cavity-nesting birds produce white eggs, as do burrow-nesting seabirds such as storm-petrels, shearwaters, and puffins. White eggs are easier for parents to locate in dark places, and there is no need for camouflage because there is relatively little risk from predators within protected cavities and burrows. The eggs of birds that build open, cup-shaped nests—sparrows, jays, and blackbirds, for example—are colored and patterned to avoid detection by predators.

The intricate swirls and speckles that decorate some bird eggs may serve functions other than camouflage. The Common Murre, a cliff-residing relative of the puffin, nests in crowded colonies and deposits its single egg on a bare rock. Experiments have shown that if the eggs of two neighboring murres are exchanged, neither will incubate the mismatched egg. Instead, each will begin searching the immediate vicinity to find its

A clutch of Great-tailed Grackle eggs blends into its surroundings.

own distinctively patterned egg. Murres also demonstrate how habitat can influence egg shape and shell thickness. On the crowded ledges where murres nest, eggs might roll off if not for their unique ergonomics. When bumped, the pear-shaped egg rotates around its pointed end rather than tumbling off the ledge. Murre eggshells are also thicker than those of most other birds, offering added protection should the egg roll against a nearby rock.

THE RIGHT NUMBER

The number of eggs in a clutch is usually the result of a compromise: The mother's biological imperative is to produce the maximum number of young without endangering her health. Maintaining the right balance is especially important for long-lived birds, such as puffins and petrels. Although they lay just one egg each year and usually spend months rearing the chick, they produce many young over the course of their lives, which often last twenty years. Some birds lay more eggs when food is abundant. Snowy Owls vary the size of their clutch per breeding season from zero to thirteen, depending upon the availability of resources.

INCUBATION

To incubate their eggs, most birds molt down, exposing a "brood patch" of skin on their breast or side. Because female land birds usually incubate the eggs, males seldom develop a brood patch. In contrast, both male and female seabirds take turns incubating their one egg. Incubation roles are reversed in some species, such as phalaropes: Only the male develops a brood patch. When sexes look similar, both usually incubate the eggs, but in species where one sex is conspicuously colored and the other wears camouflage, only the drab-plumaged bird will incubate. For example, brightly feathered male songbirds such as tanagers and most warblers rarely sit on nests, but they often feed their incubating mates. Many pairs of land birds share the responsibility, taking turns at the nest throughout the day while the other searches for food. A seabird parent, however, often spends uninterrupted weeks incubating while the mate is at sea rebuilding fat reserves and collecting food for the young. Short-tailed Shearwaters switch places every twelve to fourteen days over the course of their two-month incubation.

Clockwise from upper left: Common Loon turning its egg; nesting Killdeer; Song Sparrow nest; Common Murre with a typically pear-shaped egg

While land birds fledge young in less than two weeks, birds that live in safe habitats often incubate their eggs for longer periods. In the absence of predators, seabirds have developed remarkably long incubations. They often feed far from the nesting islands and so deliver food at great intervals—a factor that, over evolutionary time, has slowed the growth of seabird chicks. Storm-petrels incubate their eggs for thirty-eight to fifty-six days, sometimes even letting the egg chill for several days when they are delayed at sea. Following the general rule that the larger the bird, the longer the incubation, the albatross incubates its eggs for about eighty-one days. Birds that nest in open, cup-shaped nests have shorter incubations (eleven to thirteen days) than those that nest in enclosed cavities (twelve to fourteen days). The Brown-headed Cowbird, a parasitic species that lays its eggs in other birds' nests and lets the "adoptive parents" raise its young, has an incubation period of just eleven days. Born earlier, and often bigger, the chick crowds out the other young in the nest.

Parent birds have remarkable ways of maintaining uniform egg temperature. Short-tailed Shearwaters, for example, can incubate for two weeks without a break. The Emperor Penguin must contend with severe Antarctic weather, and it has a unique tactic to combat the chilling ice: It balances the egg on top of its feet. The parent can even shuffle about the colony with its egg securely in place.

The embryos of Common Murres, White Pelicans, chickens, and many more species communicate with their parents while still in the shell. The chicks make specific sounds to attract the attention of the parents, prompting them to turn the egg to prevent chilling. Equally important is to prevent overheating. Some tropical birds, such as Blue-footed Boobies, will stand over the embryos to shade them. Killdeer sometimes cool their eggs by soaking breast feathers in nearby puddles and then dripping water onto the shells.

DOWN TO EARTH

Nesting behaviors bond birds to the Earth. If it were not for the necessity of laying eggs, most seabirds would never come near land, where they are comparatively inept and vulnerable. Likewise, land birds are at greatest risk to predators and natural disasters when they are tending nests, instead of flying or foraging. The dangers associated with nesting are clearly a cost of flight, because it would be too much of a burden and too great a risk to fly with an internal clutch of developing eggs. Given the constraints of the reproductive process, birds have adapted their incubation habits to make the best of being temporarily grounded.

The Blue-footed Booby will stand over its eggs to shade them.

Marbled Godwit   {Limosa fedoa}

DATE   LOCATION

Ruddy Turnstone   {Arenaria interpres}

DATE   LOCATION

Black Turnstone   {Arenaria melanocephala}

DATE   LOCATION

Surfbird   {Aphriza virgata}

DATE   LOCATION

Red Knot   {*Calidris canutus*}

DATE   LOCATION

Sanderling   {*Calidris alba*}

DATE   LOCATION

Semipalmated Sandpiper   {*Calidris pusilla*}

DATE   LOCATION

Western Sandpiper   {*Calidris mauri*}

DATE   LOCATION

Least Sandpiper {*Calidris minutilla*}

DATE   LOCATION

White-rumped Sandpiper {*Calidris fuscicollis*}

DATE   LOCATION

Baird's Sandpiper {*Calidris bairdii*}

DATE   LOCATION

Pectoral Sandpiper {*Calidris melanotos*}

DATE   LOCATION

Sharp-tailed Sandpiper   {Calidris acuminata}

DATE   LOCATION

Purple Sandpiper   {Calidris maritima}

DATE   LOCATION

Rock Sandpiper   {Calidris ptilocnemis}

DATE   LOCATION

Dunlin   {Calidris alpina}

DATE   LOCATION

Curlew Sandpiper   { *Calidris ferruginea* }

DATE   LOCATION

Stilt Sandpiper   { *Calidris himantopus* }

DATE   LOCATION

Buff-breasted Sandpiper   { *Tryngites subruficollis* }

DATE   LOCATION

Ruff   { *Philomachus pugnax* }

DATE   LOCATION

Short-billed Dowitcher {*Limnodromus griseus*}

DATE   LOCATION

Long-billed Dowitcher {*Limnodromus scolopaceus*}

DATE   LOCATION

Common Snipe {*Gallinago gallinago*}

DATE   LOCATION

American Woodcock {*Scolopax minor*}

DATE   LOCATION

Wilson's Phalarope   {*Phalaropus tricolor*}

DATE   LOCATION

Red-necked Phalarope   {*Phalaropus lobatus*}

DATE   LOCATION

Red Phalarope   {*Phalaropus fulicaria*}

DATE   LOCATION

Gulls, Terns, and Skimmers   {Suborder Lari}

Pomarine Jaeger   {*Stercorarius pomarinus*}

DATE   LOCATION

Parasitic Jaeger {Stercorarius parasiticus}

DATE   LOCATION

Long-tailed Jaeger {Stercorarius longicaudus}

DATE   LOCATION

Laughing Gull {Larus atricilla}

DATE   LOCATION

Franklin's Gull {Larus pipixcan}

DATE   LOCATION

Little Gull

{*Larus minutus*}

DATE

LOCATION

Black-headed Gull

{*Larus ridibundus*}

DATE

LOCATION

Bonaparte's Gull

{*Larus philadelphia*}

DATE

LOCATION

Heermann's Gull

{*Larus heermanni*}

DATE

LOCATION

Mew Gull

{*Larus canus*}

DATE

LOCATION

Ring-billed Gull

{*Larus delawarensis*}

DATE

LOCATION

California Gull

{*Larus californicus*}

DATE

LOCATION

Herring Gull

{*Larus argentatus*}

DATE

LOCATION

Yellow-legged Gull   { *Larus cachinnans* }

DATE   LOCATION

Thayer's Gull   { *Larus thayeri* }

DATE   LOCATION

Iceland Gull   { *Larus glaucoides* }

DATE   LOCATION

Lesser Black-backed Gull   { *Larus fuscus* }

DATE   LOCATION

Yellow-footed Gull {*Larus livens*}

DATE LOCATION

Western Gull {*Larus occidentalis*}

DATE LOCATION

Glaucous-winged Gull {*Larus glaucescens*}

DATE LOCATION

Glaucous Gull {*Larus hyperboreus*}

DATE LOCATION

Great Black-backed Gull {Larus marinus}

DATE   LOCATION

Black-legged Kittiwake {Rissa tridactyla}

DATE   LOCATION

Red-legged Kittiwake {Rissa brevirostris}

DATE   LOCATION

Ross's Gull {Rhodostethia rosea}

DATE   LOCATION

Sabine's Gull   {*Xema sabini*}

DATE   LOCATION

Ivory Gull   {*Pagophila eburnea*}

DATE   LOCATION

Gull-billed Tern   {*Sterna nilotica*}

DATE   LOCATION

Caspian Tern   {*Sterna caspia*}

DATE   LOCATION

Royal Tern   {*Sterna maxima*}

DATE   LOCATION

Elegant Tern   {*Sterna elegans*}

DATE   LOCATION

Sandwich Tern   {*Sterna sandvicensis*}

DATE   LOCATION

Roseate Tern   {*Sterna dougallii*}

DATE   LOCATION

Common Tern

{*Sterna hirundo*}

DATE   LOCATION

Arctic Tern

{*Sterna paradisaea*}

DATE   LOCATION

Forster's Tern

{*Sterna forsteri*}

DATE   LOCATION

Least Tern

{*Sterna antillarum*}

DATE   LOCATION

Wings in the Wind

BIRDS DRIFT through the air like feathered phantoms, lifting their graceful bodies in flawless flight. Flight is the bird's characteristic feature. The sight of a bird flying is so familiar, it's easy to forget that flight is the result of a long evolutionary process. Feathered wings are adaptations of fore-limbs, and they allow birds many unique accomplishments. Over the course of millions of years, different species have customized their flying powers to their specific needs: The golden plover has endurance; the swift, speed; the albatross, power; the hummingbird, control; the falcon, aggressiveness.

Think of a bird as a flying machine: Its skeleton is the frame, its heart the motor, its lungs the cooling system, its digestive tract the fuel-treatment system, its tail the rudder and elevator, and, of course, its wings the wings. Add to these elements hollow bones; strong, flexible feathers; huge pectoral muscles; and complex circulatory and respiratory systems. All serve to keep a bird's weight low and its power output high. To further streamline operations, females have only one ovary,

A Reddish Egret spreads its wings.

and both sexes have small reproductive organs that decrease in size during the non-breeding season.

The hollow bones of a bird are honeycombed with air spaces and crisscrossed with strengthening struts. Many of its bones are fused together for rigidity and strength. In addition to the hollow bones, the great number of air sacs in a bird's body allows it to maintain constant buoyancy. Unlike the lungs of a mammal, in which the volume of air changes with each inhalation and exhalation, avian lungs maintain a uniform volume of air. The lungs inflate but do not deflate; they hold air. If the lungs were to inflate and deflate with every breath, a bird in flight would continually gain and lose altitude.

Muscles constitute approximately one half of a bird's total body weight. Bulky muscles are concentrated near the center of gravity, contributing to stability in flight. The largest, the breast muscles, provide the powerful downstroke of the wing and bear most of the burden of supporting the bird in the air. Besides these, there are many other small wing muscles that allow a bird to control its flight.

THE FUNCTION OF FEATHERS

Feathers serve a variety of functions: They enable flight, conserve heat, repel water, provide camouflage, and attract mates. Each feather consists of a tapered shaft, the rachis, with a flexible vane on either side. The inner and outer vanes carried by the rachis are composed of a row of barbs, arranged side by side. Each barb contains many tiny branches, called barbules. The exposed base of the shaft is called the calamus, or quill. Feathers are classified according to their functions. In birds of all sizes, there are six commonly recognized types of feathers: contour, semiplume, filoplume, down, powder down, and bristle.

Contour feathers include the feathers of the outer body, as well as those of the wings and tail. They range in length and thickness from large, stiff flight feathers to softer, more delicate feathers that shape the body. Contour feathers used for flight are known as remiges (in the wing) and rectrices (in the tail). Remiges allow the bird to travel wide expanses; rectrices are mainly involved with steering and balancing. Used as a rudder, they allow the bird to twist and turn in flight. They also act as an efficient brake before landing.

Semiplume feathers insulate and provide flexibility at constricted areas, such as the base of the wings. Semiplumes are usually hidden beneath the contour feathers and are small and often white.

Filoplume feathers are hairlike structures that grow in circles around the base

An American Avocet takes flight.

of contour or down feathers. They usually stand up like hairs and are made up of a thin rachis with a few short barbs or barbules at the tip. Smaller than semiplumes, filoplumes are about half the length of the covering contour feathers.

Down feathers make up the underplumage of a bird, and their main function also seems to be insulation. Each down feather has a quill and a soft head of fluffly barbs. These feathers are especially numerous in ducks and other water birds. Chicks of some species are covered with down when they hatch.

Unlike other feathers, powder downs grow continuously. Instead of being molted, their tips disintegrate into a powdery substance. These feathers grow in dense, yellowish patches on the breast, belly, or flanks of herons and bitterns. In other birds powder downs are thinly distributed throughout the plumage.

A Broad-tailed Hummingbird flits on a figwort flower.

Not all species have bristles. They have a stiff, tapered rachis and few, if any, barbs. Bristles are found on the head or neck, often around the mouth or on the eyelids. In some insect-eaters, bristles found on the face and around the mouth are thought to act as funnels, helping the birds to scoop insects out of the air. Long facial bristles in owls, which tend to be farsighted, aid them in sensing nearby objects. Woodpeckers have bristle feathers over their nostrils that act as filters for the dust produced when they drill holes in trees.

The Hummingbird: Master of the Air

The human eye cannot detect how rapidly a hummingbird's wings beat. The most maneuverable of all fliers, hummingbirds hover motionless, fly backward, shift sideways, pivot around on a stationary axis, and achieve practically full speed the instant they take wing. No other bird can do all these things. There isn't a bird of prey that even attempts to catch a hummingbird in flight.

Only seabirds, such as albatrosses and shearwaters, can cross miles of ocean with ease; only hawks, eagles, and condors can soar over vast mountain ranges, using thermals and wind currents deflected by mountains, cliffs, or buildings. Smaller birds, such as robins, warblers, and sparrows, can glide, but they cannot soar in updrafts over land or gusts over sea. These birds must generate their own energy for flight, which is achieved by beating the wings in what is called flapping flight. Regardless, the exceptional powers of flight have enabled birds to colonize any and all terrestrial regions, and to substitute distance for concealment.

Bridled Tern

{*Sterna anaethetus*}

DATE

LOCATION

Sooty Tern

{*Sterna fuscata*}

DATE

LOCATION

White-winged Tern

{*Chlidonias leucopterus*}

DATE

LOCATION

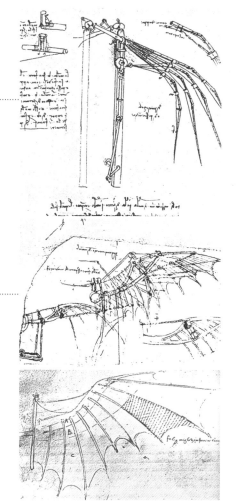

Black Tern

{*Chlidonias niger*}

DATE

LOCATION

Humans have always envied birds' ability to fly.

Gulls, Terns, and Skimmers (cont'd)   {Suborder Lari}

Brown Noddy   {*Anous stolidus*}

DATE   LOCATION

Black Skimmer   {*Rynchops niger*}

DATE   LOCATION

Murres, Auks, and Puffins   {Suborder Alcae}

Dovekie   {*Alle alle*}

DATE   LOCATION

Common Murre   {*Uria aalge*}

DATE   LOCATION

Thick-billed Murre   { *Uria lomvia* }

DATE   LOCATION

Razorbill   { *Alca torda* }

DATE   LOCATION

Black Guillemot   { *Cepphus grylle* }

DATE   LOCATION

Pigeon Guillemot   { *Cepphus columba* }

DATE   LOCATION

Marbled Murrelet {Brachyramphus marmoratus}

DATE   LOCATION

Kittlitz's Murrelet {Brachyramphus brevirostris}

DATE   LOCATION

Xantus's Murrelet {Synthliboramphus hypoleucus}

DATE   LOCATION

Craveri's Murrelet {Synthliboramphus craveri}

DATE   LOCATION

Ancient Murrelet
{ Synthliboramphus antiquus }

DATE

LOCATION

Cassin's Auklet
{ Ptychoramphus aleuticus }

DATE

LOCATION

Parakeet Auklet
{ Cyclorrhynchus psittacula }

DATE

LOCATION

Least Auklet
{ Aethia pusilla }

DATE

LOCATION

Whiskered Auklet   {*Aethia pygmaea*}

DATE   LOCATION

Crested Auklet   {*Aethia cristatella*}

DATE   LOCATION

Rhinoceros Auklet   {*Cerorhinca monocerata*}

DATE   LOCATION

Tufted Puffin   {*Fratercula cirrhata*}

DATE   LOCATION

Atlantic Puffin   {*Fratercula arctica*}

DATE   LOCATION

Horned Puffin   {*Fratercula corniculata*}

DATE   LOCATION

PIGEONS AND DOVES   {Order Columbiformes}

Rock Dove   {*Columba livia*}

DATE   LOCATION

White-crowned Pigeon   {*Columba leucocephala*}

DATE   LOCATION

*A*nd again he sent forth the dove out of the ark; And the dove came in to him in the evening; and, lo, in her mouth was an olive leaf pluckt off: so Noah knew that the waters were abated from off the earth. And he stayed yet other seven days; and sent forth the dove; which returned not again unto him any more.

(Genesis 8:6–12)

Band-tailed Pigeon   {Columba fasciata}

DATE   LOCATION

Eurasian Collared-Dove   {Streptopelia decaocto}

DATE   LOCATION

Spotted Dove   {Streptopelia chinensis}

DATE   LOCATION

White-winged Dove   {Zenaida asiatica}

DATE   LOCATION

Mourning Dove {*Zenaida macroura*}

DATE LOCATION

The time of the singing of birds is come . . . Arise, my love, my fair one, and come away. O my dove, that art in the clefts of the rock, in the secret places of the stairs, let me see thy countenance, let me hear thy voice; for sweet is thy voice, and thy countenance is comely.

(Song of Solomon 2:11–14)

Inca Dove {*Columbina inca*}

DATE LOCATION

Common Ground-Dove {*Columbia passerina*}

DATE LOCATION

Ruddy Ground-Dove {*Columbina talpacoti*}

DATE LOCATION

PIGEONS AND DOVES *(cont'd)*   {Order Columbiformes}

White-tipped Dove   {*Leptotila verreauxi*}

DATE   LOCATION

PARROTS   {Order Psittaciformes}

Budgerigar   {*Melopsittacus undulatus*}

DATE   LOCATION

Monk Parakeet   {*Myiopsitta monachus*}

DATE   LOCATION

Canary-winged Parakeet   {*Brotogeris versicolurus*}

DATE   LOCATION

Red-crowned Parrot

{ *Amazona viridigenalis* }

DATE

LOCATION

Cuckoos

{ Order Cuculiformes }

Black-billed Cuckoo

{ *Coccyzus erythropthalmus* }

DATE

LOCATION

Yellow-billed Cuckoo

{ *Coccyzus americanus* }

DATE

LOCATION

Mangrove Cuckoo

{ *Coccyzus minor* }

DATE

LOCATION

CUCKOOS *(cont'd)* {Order Cuculiformes}

Lesser Roadrunner {Geococcyx velox}

DATE   LOCATION

Greater Roadrunner {Geococcyx californianus}

DATE   LOCATION

Smooth-billed Ani {Crotophaga ani}

DATE   LOCATION

Groove-billed Ani {Crotophaga sulcirostris}

DATE   LOCATION

OWLS {Order Strigiformes}

Barn Owl {*Tyto alba*}

DATE LOCATION

Flammulated Owl {*Otus flammeolus*}

DATE LOCATION

Eastern Screech-Owl {*Otus asio*}

DATE LOCATION

Western Screech-Owl {*Otus kennicottii*}

DATE LOCATION

Whiskered Screech-Owl

{*Otus trichopsis*}

DATE

LOCATION

Great Horned Owl

{*Bubo virginianus*}

DATE

LOCATION Elkhart R. flood plain near dam, Goshen

Snowy Owl

{*Nyctea scandiaca*}

DATE

LOCATION

Northern Hawk-Owl

{*Surnia ulula*}

DATE

LOCATION

Northern Pygmy-Owl   { *Glaucidium gnoma* }

DATE   LOCATION

Ferruginous Pygmy-Owl   { *Glaucidium brasilianum* }

DATE   LOCATION

Elf Owl   { *Micrathene whitneyi* }

DATE   LOCATION

Burrowing Owl   { *Speotyto cunicularia* }

DATE   LOCATION

Spotted Owl   {*Strix occidentalis*}

DATE   LOCATION

Barred Owl   {*Strix varia*}

DATE   LOCATION

Great Gray Owl   {*Strix nebulosa*}

DATE   LOCATION

Long-eared Owl   {*Asio otus*}

DATE   LOCATION

The Bird in Mythology

BIRDS NAVIGATE the heavens, divine messengers of the gods. Soaring above the Earth, they are granted a breadth of vision that humans can only imagine. In Egypt, when a person died, it was essential that birds be buried with the corpse, to ensure the safe transport of the released soul to the spirit realm. Many religions maintain that meditation frees the spirit, which then flies to its sacred source. In certain cultures, shamans don elaboratedly feathered garments or graphically beaked masks, so that, by appearing like birds, they will, in their trances, be granted divine knowledge. In Islam, the maternal dove calls souls to prayer.

OMNIPOTENT EAGLES

The eagle, known in Greek and Roman mythology as the carrier of celestial fire, bore in its claws Zeus's lightning bolts. In the Indian epic *Rāmāyana*, Vishnu rode

Northern Hawk Owl: Owls are considered the most sagacious of birds.

Garuda (the eagle) as his divine mount after the bird stole the immortality of the gods. Egyptian and Assyrian cultures believed the sun was endowed with the wings of an eagle, its rays represented by twelve feathers. Wandering Aztecs looked to an eagle, which they called the "winged wolf" for its grand flight and dauntless courage, to show them where to settle: When an eagle, snake in mouth, landed on a cactus tree, they considered it an omen, ceased their searching, and established their capital, Tenochtitlán—today, Mexico City.

Negative myths also came to be associated with eagles. Positive qualities of courage and power could, when pushed to the extreme, turn into oppression and pride, leading to vain, self-righteous acts. The legend of Icarus cautions against excessive ambition, and Christians likened the eagle's ability to swoop down and dig its sharp claws into weaker prey to the devil's greedy ravishing of human hearts.

OMINOUS RAVENS

Black, raucous, and scavenging, ravens and crows have been made into symbols of evil. Legend has it that the raven was originally a white bird, but an angry Apollo turned it black because it reported a nymph's infidelity. The foreboding black plumage of ravens and crows, along with their taste for carrion, links them with doom and death—the most popular example of this undoubtably being Edgar Allen Poe's *The Raven*. But the raven's canniness has also earned it respect. Unlike eagles, ravens do not look majestic or fierce, but they excel in wit, daring, and play. They also thrive anywhere, from the tundra to cities. Among the peoples of the Pacific Northwest, the raven is the great creator. A myth of the Queen Charlotte Islands in Canada tells of the raven discovering a clam full of frightened people, the residue of a great flood. The raven encourages them to leave the shell and introduces them to the islands. In the Old Testament, it is a dove that brings Noah an olive branch and the news of land nearby.

The goddess Aphrodite often rode on the back of a swan, or in a chariot pulled by a brace of swans. Zeus took the form of the swan to seduce the lovely mortal Leda. From their coupling, four children were born: Clytemnestra, Castor, Pollux, and Helen.

Eggs were highly valued because they signified fertility, the crucial concern of early peoples trying to survive from one year to the next. In pre-Christian millenia, goddesses were depicted as fertile birds, with forward-thrusting breasts and enlarged buttocks that cradled eggs. These bird-goddesses carried the essence of life within themselves.

Clockwise from upper left: Bathers with Birds, from the Tomba della Caccia e della Pesca in Tarquinia, Etruscan era, Italy; Dove Bearing Olive Branch, detail from "Noah in His Ark," thirteenth century, Germany; Birds in Papyrus Marshes, detail of a painting from the tomb of Nebamun, Egypt; Roman fresco, "Leda and the Swan," Italy

Page 120:
The American Crow, by John James Audubon

Short-eared Owl   {*Asio flammeus*}

DATE   LOCATION

Boreal Owl   {*Aegolius funereus*}

DATE   LOCATION

Northern Saw-whet Owl   {*Aegolius acadicus*}

DATE   LOCATION

NIGHTJARS   {Order Caprimulgiformes}

Lesser Nighthawk   {*Chordeiles acutipennis*}

DATE   LOCATION

Common Nighthawk {Chordeiles minor}

DATE LOCATION

Antillean Nighthawk {Chordeiles gundlachii}

DATE LOCATION

Pauraque {Nyctidromus albicollis}

DATE LOCATION

Common Poorwill {Phalaenoptilus nuttallii}

DATE LOCATION

Chuck-will's-widow   { Caprimulgus carolinensis }

DATE   LOCATION

> *H*ark! that's the nightingale,
> Telling the selfsame tale
> Her song told when this ancient earth was young:
> So echoes answered when her song was sung
> In the first wooded vale.
>
> We call it love and pain
> The passion of her strain;
> And yet we little understand or know;
> Why should it not be rather joy that so
> Throbs in each throbbing vein?

Buff-collared Nightjar   { Caprimulgus ridgwayi }

DATE   LOCATION

PAIN OR JOY

Christina Rossetti

Whip-poor-will   { Caprimulgus vociferus }

DATE *Summer 1968*   LOCATION *Bradford woods, Morgan Co IN, (heard but not sighted)*

SWIFTS AND HUMMINGBIRDS   { Order Apodiformes }

Black Swift   { Cypseloides niger }

DATE   LOCATION

TO A SKYLARK

Hail to thee, blithe Spirit!
Bird thou never wert,
That from Heaven, or near it,
Pourest thy full heart
In profuse strains of unpremeditated art.

Higher still and higher
From the earth thou springest
Like a cloud of fire;
The blue deep thou wingest,
And singing still dost soar, and soaring ever singest.

In the golden lightning
Of the sunken sun,
O'er which clouds are bright'ning,
Thou dost float and run;
Like an unbodied joy whose race is just begun.

The pale purple even
Melts around thy flight;
Like a star of Heaven,
In the broad daylight
Thou art unseen, but yet I hear thy shrill delight,

Keen as are the arrows
Of that silver sphere,
Whose intense lamp narrows
In the white dawn clear
Until we hardly see—we feel that it is there.

All the earth and air
With thy voice is loud,
As, when night is bare,
From one lonely cloud
The moon rains out her beams, and Heaven is overflowed.

What thou art we know not;
What is most like thee?
From rainbow clouds there flow not
Drops so bright to see
As from thy presence showers a rain of melody.

Like a Poet hidden
In the light of thought,
Singing hymns unbidden,
Till the world is wrought
To sympathy with hopes and fears it heeded not:

Like a high-born maiden
In a palace-tower,
Soothing her love-laden
Soul in secret hour
With music sweet as love, which overflows her bower:

Like a glow-worm golden
In a dell of dew,
Scattered unbeholden
Its aëreal hue
Among the flowers and grass, which screen it from
the view!

Like a rose embowered
In its own green leaves,
By warm winds deflowered,
Till the scent it gives
Makes faint with too much sweet those heavy-winged
thieves:

Sound of vernal showers
On the twinkling grass,
Rain-awakened flowers,
All that ever was
Joyous, and clear, and fresh, thy music doth surpass:

Teach us, Sprite or Bird,
What sweet thoughts are thine:
I have never heard
Praise of love or wine
That panted forth a flood of rapture so divine.

Chorus Hymeneal,
Or triumphal chant,
Matched with thine would be all
But an empty vaunt,
A thing wherein we feel there is some hidden want.

What objects are the fountains
Of thy happy strain?
What fields, or waves, or mountains?
What shapes of sky or plain?
What love of thine own kind? what ignorance of pain?

With thy clear keen joyance
Langour cannot be:
Shadow of annoyance
Never came near thee:
Thou lovest—but ne'er knew love's sad satiety.

Waking or asleep,
Thou of death must deem
Things more true and deep
Than we mortals dream,
Or how could thy notes flow in such a crystal stream?

We look before and after,
And pine for what is not:
Our sincerest laughter
With some pain is fraught;
Our sweetest songs are those that tell of saddest thought.

Yet if we could scorn
Hate, and pride, and fear;
If we were things born
Not to shed a tear,
I know not how thy joy we ever should come near.

Better than all measures
Of delightful sound,
Better than all treasures
That in books are found,
Thy skill to poet were, thou scorner of the ground!

Teach me half the gladness
That thy brain must know,
Such harmonious madness
From my lips would flow
The world should listen then—as I am listening now.

PERCY BYSSHE SHELLEY

Chimney Swift

{Chaetura pelagica}

DATE

LOCATION

Vaux's Swift

{Chaetura vauxi}

DATE

LOCATION

White-throated Swift

{Aeronautes saxatalis}

DATE

LOCATION

Broad-billed Hummingbird

{Cynanthus latirostris}

DATE

LOCATION

White-eared Hummingbird   {*Hylocharis leucotis*}

DATE   LOCATION

Berylline Hummingbird   {*Amazilia beryllina*}

DATE   LOCATION

Buff-bellied Hummingbird   {*Amazilia yucatanensis*}

DATE   LOCATION

Violet-crowned Hummingbird   {*Amazilia violiceps*}

DATE   LOCATION

Blue-throated Hummingbird {*Lampornis clemenciae*}

DATE   LOCATION

Magnificent Hummingbird {*Eugenes fulgens*}

DATE   LOCATION

Plain-capped Starthroat {*Heliomaster constantii*}

DATE   LOCATION

Bahama Woodstar {*Calliphlox evelynae*}

DATE   LOCATION

Lucifer Hummingbird　　　　　　　{ *Calothorax lucifer* }

DATE　　　　　　　　　　　　　　　LOCATION

Ruby-throated Hummingbird　　　　{ *Archilochus colubris* }

DATE　　　　　　　　　　　　　　　LOCATION

Black-chinned Hummingbird　　　　{ *Archilochus alexandri* }

DATE　　　　　　　　　　　　　　　LOCATION

Anna's Hummingbird　　　　　　　{ *Calypte anna* }

DATE　　　　　　　　　　　　　　　LOCATION

Costa's Hummingbird　　　　　{Calypte costae}

DATE　　　　　LOCATION

Calliope Hummingbird　　　　　{Stellula calliope}

DATE　　　　　LOCATION

Broad-tailed Hummingbird　　　　　{Selasphorus platycercus}

DATE　　　　　LOCATION

Rufous Hummingbird　　　　　{Selasphorus rufus}

DATE　　　　　LOCATION

Allen's Hummingbird

{ *Selasphorus sasin* }

DATE

LOCATION

TROGONS

{ Order Trogoniformes }

Elegant Trogon

{ *Trogon elegans* }

DATE

LOCATION

Eared Trogon

{ *Euptilotis neoxenus* }

DATE

LOCATION

KINGFISHERS

{ Order Coraciiformes }

Ringed Kingfisher

{ *Ceryle torquata* }

DATE

LOCATION

Belted Kingfisher

{Ceryle alcyon}

DATE 4-1-03

LOCATION JJ Audubon S.P. Henderson KY (not first)

Green Kingfisher

{Chloroceryle americana}

DATE

LOCATION

WOODPECKERS {Order Piciformes}

Lewis's Woodpecker

{Melanerpes lewis}

DATE

LOCATION

Red-headed Woodpecker

{Melanerpes erythrocephalus}

DATE 4-2-03

LOCATION Land between Lakes NRA, KY (not first)

Acorn Woodpecker

{ *Melanerpes formicivorus* }

DATE

LOCATION

Gila Woodpecker

{ *Melanerpes uropygialis* }

DATE

LOCATION

Golden-fronted Woodpecker

{ *Melanerpes aurifrons* }

DATE

LOCATION

Red-bellied Woodpecker

{ *Melanerpes carolinus* }

DATE

LOCATION

Yellow-bellied Sapsucker   {Sphyrapicus varius}

DATE   LOCATION

Red-naped Sapsucker   {Sphyrapicus nuchalis}

DATE   LOCATION

Red-breasted Sapsucker   {Sphyrapicus ruber}

DATE   LOCATION

Williamson's Sapsucker   {Sphyrapicus thyroideus}

DATE   LOCATION

Ladder-backed Woodpecker   { *Picoides scalaris* }

DATE   LOCATION

Nuttall's Woodpecker   { *Picoides nuttallii* }

DATE   LOCATION

Downy Woodpecker   { *Picoides pubescens* }

DATE   LOCATION

Hairy Woodpecker   { *Picoides villosus* }

DATE   LOCATION

Strickland's Woodpecker

{*Picoides stricklandi*}

DATE

LOCATION

Red-cockaded Woodpecker

{*Picoides borealis*}

DATE

LOCATION

White-headed Woodpecker

{*Picoides albolarvatus*}

DATE

LOCATION

Three-toed Woodpecker

{*Picoides tridactylus*}

DATE

LOCATION

Vision

WHAT MAKES a bird a bird? Its ability to fly? Other creatures fly—thousands of species of insects, many mammals, even some fish. And there are many flightless birds. Feathers? Perhaps. Feathers, which are probably highly evolved hair or scale structures, do characterize most birds (though the scales on some insects appear very featherlike). But most likely it is vision that distinguishes a bird. In virtually all other classes of animals, some species have "devolved" their sense of vision, but there is no blind bird species. In many aspects, birds are the most visual of all creatures. Their highly evolved vision plays a crucial role in nearly every aspect of their survival. It is essential for migration, courtship, foraging, identification of young, territorial defense, and protection against predators.

Though much studied, avian vision is little understood. In relation to the size of their heads, most birds have very large eyes. Within the eye, attached to the retina near the optic nerve, is a structure called the "pecten," a pleated organ containing many blood vessels, whose function still eludes ornithologists. Though many theories have been postulated, the current best guess is that the pecten supplies nutrition and oxygen to the avian retina.

The eyes of birds, unlike those of mammals, are receptive to the ultraviolet and near-ultraviolet spectra. Human eyes absorb UV light, but in avian retinas the peak of sensitivity is in the near-UV range. Some birds are able to discern patterns totally invisible to humans. These patterns may aid in the recognition of species, which to people appear to have identical plumage, such as many tropical hummingbirds or high-altitude tapaculos. The ability to detect patterns of UV may also assist birds, such as sunbirds and hummingbirds, in search of nectar.

An attentive Tricolored Heron

The Burrowing Owl can rotate its head about 270 degrees.

VISION IN BIRDS OF PREY

Birds of prey fall into two basic categories: diurnal species—hawks, eagles, and falcons; and nocturnal species—owls and nightjars. Both groups have specific adaptations to best suit their predatory needs. For example, diurnal birds such as buteos have extremely sharp sight, up to three times as acute as that of mammals, and broad, long wings built for effortless soaring at considerable altitudes. Most diurnal bird species also have extremely acute color vision. The density of their retinal cones—the receptors responsible for color vision—is nearly twice that of humans or other mammals. Because of this, diurnal birds are probably better able to recognize minute differences in pattern or color in their surrounding environment. And most species of diurnal birds of prey possess high densities of both rods and cones in their retinas, and so can perceive great detail at considerable distance. This keen vision enables them to survey intently the world below and watch for any movement that could signal a tender morsel. The eyes of buteos are on the sides of the head but toward the front, allowing them good binocular vision, especially in the forward sector, and excellent depth perception, which is advantageous in a dive. Moreover, their eyeballs are able to rotate in their sockets, permitting quick visual acquisition of prey below.

Nocturnal birds have a different set of adaptations for their forays. For their extremely accurate vision, they have an especially high density of retinal rods—

Wood Duck   *Brown Pelican*   *Osprey*

black-and-white light receptors—enabling them to detect movement and hunt in near-darkness. Even by bird standards, owls, for example, have very large eyes that collect even more light in dim conditions. Their eyes are situated in the front of their face, but the eyeballs are not mobile in the sockets. Since owls have excellent binocular vision directly in front of their heads but cannot move their eyes from side to side, there is extreme mobility in their necks: Owls can rotate their heads about 270 degrees in order to face potential prey. Because their eyes are surrounded by a round, concave face, which serves as a dish that concentrates sound to the ears, by just aiming their head in the right direction, owls benefit from a simultaneous double-detection system for prey. But owls are not able to see in total darkness. In that circumstance, hearing becomes the primary cue, enabling owls to successfully capture prey even if they do not have their dinner in sight.

Prey Species

Just as birds of prey need excellent vision to hunt, other species, such as ducks, doves, warblers, and sparrows, need to rely on sharp-sightedness to defend themselves. Prey species have interesting adaptations to increase their chances of survival. Groups of birds, such as shorebirds and waterfowl, have very acute vision and are especially adept at detecting moving silhouettes in the sky. Their immediate defense is often to hunker down into their surroundings. Then they may take flight all at once, in the hopes of confusing the approaching predator. Most prey species have their primary cone of binocular vision—the best sector for depth and movement perception—situated above and to the front in their field of view, enabling them to detect distant predators approaching in their forward visual hemisphere.

The American Woodcock, however, has little or no chance for advance warning in the forward hemisphere, because it spends most of its time probing deep into dirt, often surrounded by dense vegetation. The greatest threat for woodcocks is from directly above and slightly behind their head. Appropriately, their eyes are set on the sides of the head and somewhat above the center, giving them their cone of binocular vision to the top and behind the head—exactly where they most need it.

Some species of pond ducks and ground-feeding doves have their eyes set so widely apart on the head that they practically have no binocular vision at all. Instead, they are particularly adept at sensing motion across their two separate hemispheres of view. In essence, these species are able to scan twice as much sky at once, with the penalty being a lack of depth perception.

LIVING COLOR

With their extremely sharp eyesight, it is only natural that distinguishing colors is crucial to their day-to-day survival. Visual cues, including color patterns, shapes, and unanticipated movement, abound in their environment, aiding birds in foraging; the recognition of their mates and their young; the defense of their territory against other birds; and the evaluation of threats to themselves and their young. The riot of colors seen in the plumage of similar-size and -shape groups, such as wood warblers, tanagers, sunbirds, and hummingbirds, facilitates recognition of potential territorial interlopers of the same species, and ensures that mating occurs only with a chosen mate of the opposite sex—and the same species!

Some groups of birds that feed on nectar, such as hummingbirds, are particularly attracted to bright objects, especially red ones, as they search their territories for flowers in full bloom. A tiny male Calliope Hummingbird, quickly recognizing a competitor by his red-striped gorget near a brighty colored nectar-laden flower, defensively sallies forth in order to ensure his and his clutch's survival. The vivid hues in nature, signaling both the presence of a territorial interloper and the colorful flower as a source of food, are cues quickly put together by the male hummingbird—just one example of how the colors of nature that add so much to our enjoyment of the natural world, are in fact crucial to the survival of the amazingly visual creatures we call birds.

Black-backed Woodpecker   {Picoides arcticus}

DATE   LOCATION

Northern Flicker   {Colaptes auratus}

DATE   LOCATION

Gilded Flicker   {Colaptes chrysoides}

DATE   LOCATION

Pileated Woodpecker   {Dryocopus pileatus}

DATE   LOCATION

3-28-03   (spotted nest)   Noblesville IN - River Trail

11-   02   ,,   ,,   River Trail

4-01-03   Audubon S.P. KY (2 seen)

Northern Beardless-Tyrannulet

{ *Camptostoma imberbe* }

DATE

LOCATION

Olive-sided Flycatcher

{ *Contopus borealis* }

DATE

LOCATION

Greater Pewee

{ *Contopus pertinax* }

DATE

LOCATION

Western Wood-Pewee

{ *Contopus sordidulus* }

DATE

LOCATION

Eastern Wood-Pewee   { *Contopus virens* }

DATE   LOCATION

Yellow-bellied Flycatcher   { *Empidonax flaviventris* }

DATE   LOCATION

Acadian Flycatcher   { *Empidonax virescens* }

DATE   LOCATION

Alder Flycatcher   { *Empidonax alnorum* }

DATE   LOCATION

Willow Flycatcher   {*Empidonax traillii*}

DATE   LOCATION

Least Flycatcher   {*Empidonax minimus*}

DATE   LOCATION

Hammond's Flycatcher   {*Empidonax hammondii*}

DATE   LOCATION

Dusky Flycatcher   {*Empidonax oberholseri*}

DATE   LOCATION

Gray Flycatcher {*Empidonax wrightii*}

DATE   LOCATION

Pacific-slope Flycatcher {*Empidonax difficilis*}

DATE   LOCATION

Cordilleran Flycatcher {*Empidonax occidentalis*}

DATE   LOCATION

Black Phoebe {*Sayornis nigricans*}

DATE   LOCATION

Eastern Phoebe   {*Sayornis phoebe*}

DATE   LOCATION

Say's Phoebe   {*Sayornis saya*}

DATE   LOCATION

Vermilion Flycatcher   {*Pyrocephalus rubinus*}

DATE   LOCATION

Dusky-capped Flycatcher   {*Myiarchus tuberculifer*}

DATE   LOCATION

Ash-throated Flycatcher   {*Myiarchus cinerascens*}

DATE   LOCATION

Nutting's Flycatcher   {*Myiarchus nuttingi*}

DATE   LOCATION

Great Crested Flycatcher   {*Myiarchus crinitus*}

DATE   LOCATION

Brown-crested Flycatcher   {*Myiarchus tyrannulus*}

DATE   LOCATION

Tyrant-Flycatchers (cont'd) {Family Tyrannidae}

La Sagra's Flycatcher {*Myiarchus sagrae*}

DATE   LOCATION

Great Kiskadee {*Pitangus sulphuratus*}

DATE   LOCATION

Sulphur-bellied Flycatcher {*Myiodynastes luteiventris*}

DATE   LOCATION

Tropical Kingbird {*Tyrannus melancholicus*}

DATE   LOCATION

Couch's Kingbird

DATE

{ *Tyrannus couchii* }

LOCATION

Cassin's Kingbird

DATE

{ *Tyrannus vociferans* }

LOCATION

Western Kingbird

DATE

{ *Tyrannus verticalis* }

LOCATION

Eastern Kingbird

DATE

{ *Tyrannus tyrannus* }

LOCATION

Gray Kingbird

{ *Tyrannus dominicensis* }

DATE

LOCATION

Loggerhead Kingbird

{ *Tyrannus caudifasciatus* }

DATE

LOCATION

Scissor-tailed Flycatcher

{ *Tyrannus forficatus* }

DATE

LOCATION

Fork-tailed Flycatcher

{ *Tyrannus savana* }

DATE

LOCATION

Rose-throated Becard   {Pachyramphus aglaiae}

DATE   LOCATION

Larks   {Family Alaudidae}

Sky Lark   {Alauda arvensis}

DATE   LOCATION

Horned Lark   {Eremophila alpestris}

DATE   LOCATION

Swallows   {Family Hirundinidae}

Purple Martin   {Progne subis}

DATE   LOCATION

Swallows (cont'd)   {Family Hirundinidae}

Tree Swallow   {*Tachycineta bicolor*}

DATE 4-03-03   LOCATION Muscatatuck NWR Jackson Co, IN

Violet-green Swallow   {*Tachycineta thalassina*}

DATE   LOCATION

Bahama Swallow   {*Tachycineta cyaneoviridis*}

DATE   LOCATION

Northern Rough-winged Swallow   {*Stelgidopteryx serripennis*}

DATE   LOCATION

Bank Swallow

{ Riparia riparia }

DATE   LOCATION

Cliff Swallow

{ Hirundo pyrrhonota }

DATE   LOCATION

Cave Swallow

{ Hirundo fulva }

DATE   LOCATION

Barn Swallow

{ Hirundo rustica }

DATE   LOCATION

As the bird by wandering, as the
swallow by flying, so the curse
causeless shall not come.

(Proverbs 26:2)

Jays and Crows   {Family Corvidae}

Gray Jay   {*Perisoreus canadensis*}

DATE   LOCATION

Steller's Jay   {*Cyanocitta stelleri*}

DATE   LOCATION

Blue Jay   {*Cyanocitta cristata*}

DATE   LOCATION

Green Jay   {*Cyanocorax yncas*}

DATE   LOCATION

Brown Jay

{ *Cyanocorax morio* }

DATE   LOCATION

Florida Scrub-Jay

{ *Aphelocoma coerulescens* }

DATE   LOCATION

Island Scrub-Jay

{ *Aphelocoma insularis* }

DATE   LOCATION

Western Scrub-Jay

{ *Aphelocoma californica* }

DATE   LOCATION

Jays and Crows *(cont'd)*   {Family Corvidae}

Mexican Jay   {*Aphelocoma ultramarina*}

DATE   LOCATION

Pinyon Jay   {*Gymnorhinus cyanocephalus*}

DATE   LOCATION

Clark's Nutcracker   {*Nucifraga columbiana*}

DATE   LOCATION

Black-billed Magpie   {*Pica pica*}

DATE   LOCATION

Song

BIRDS PRODUCE an astonishing range of vocalizations, from the deep, guttural *croak* of the Common Raven, to the whistled *fee-bee* of the Black-capped Chickadee, to the bright *sweet-sweet-sweet-sweet* of the Yellow Warbler, to the caroling *cheer-up, cheerily* of the American Robin. But what makes a song, a song? A traditional, arbitrary distinction exists between "songs" and "calls." In general, songs are long, complex vocalizations usually produced by males in the breeding season (although many tropical species sing year-round). They consist of distinct phrases that are composed of syllables. Upon finer inspection, the syllables consist of elements. Depending on the species and individual bird singing, phrases and syllables can be short and simple, or long and complex in acoustical structure. Many species have repertoires of more than one song type. Calls, theoretically, are short, simple vocalizations of either sex given throughout the year. Calls convey specific messages: alarm, distress, hunger; also contact between mates, family, and flock members, for example. In reality, the distinction between songs and calls and the differences in their acoustical structure are ambiguous, often revealing more about what is considered pleasing to human ears.

HOW BIRDS PRODUCE SONG

Birdsong begins in the bird brain. Nerve impulses fire in the forebrain and travel through an intricate neural pathway to the muscles in the syrinx (the bird's vocal organ) that control sound. Research on mockingbirds, known for their complex song repertoires, suggests that hundreds of neurons store unique song syllables. In canaries, nuclei in the motor pathway grow in size when yearling birds learn to sing in their first spring, disintegrate when birds stop singing in the fall, and increase

Least Tern Chick

again the following spring when birds add new syllables to their repertoires. Research on Zebra Finches has revealed that male songbirds have larger and more song nuclei than do female songbirds—not surprising considering that in most species males do the singing. Sexual differences in song nuclei develop as birds age; experiments have shown that the nuclei of young females can be masculinized with sex hormone treatments. Moreover, species with large song repertoires have larger song nuclei than do species with small repertoires, suggesting a direct relationship between brain size and ability throughout the evolution of singing in birds.

Birdsong, initiated in the brain, is emitted by the syrinx, an organ unique to birds. Humans can produce only one sound at a time with their larynx, but songbirds can produce two sounds at once with their syrinx. By mixing two voices, the syrinx gives songbirds their ability to produce complex, beautiful sounds.

Song Formation

As with all complex behaviors, song does not appear fully formed when a bird reaches maturity. Song takes time to develop—songbirds learn to sing just as humans learn to speak. In general, songbirds are born with an internal template defining the basic features of their species's song. During a critical learning period, when they may hear many species' songs, young songbirds memorize only those songs that match their templates, then store them for future use. Testosterone begins circulating in yearling male songbirds in their first spring, and they begin to sing. Matching their songs to those they memorized, yearlings progress through a subsong period, when songs are given quietly and are highly variable in acoustical structure, to a plastic song period, when songs become louder and increasingly structured. During song crystallization, the yearlings' songs are perfected.

Lazuli Buntings provide an interesting case study of song learning. Yearling males arrive at the breeding grounds with species-typical, but plastic, songs. These songs are short, lack acoustically complex syllables, and are variable in syllable structure between sequential songs. Shortly after their arrival, yearlings begin copying the songs of older neighboring males, using them as song tutors. Some yearlings copy syllables from just one song tutor; other yearlings may copy syllables from as many as ten different tutors. Within days to weeks, yearlings incorporate the copied syllables into a single, crystallized song, which they retain for life. A result of this song learning is that it gives rise to the development of song neighborhoods or dialects, whereby the songs of neighbors are more alike than those of geographically distant males. Similar to the way people from Boston speak

Clockwise from top left: Yellow-headed Blackbird; Chestnut-collared Longspur; Arctic Warbler; Western Meadowlark; Yellow Warbler; White-throated Sparrow; Common Yellowthroat; Red-winged Blackbird; House Wren

differently from people from Atlanta, songbirds within the same species—for example, White-crowned Sparrows, Brown-headed Cowbirds, and Indigo Buntings—may sing differently depending on where they live.

The general strategy of song learning is similar across species, but patterns of learning vary greatly. Some species learn early in life, others throughout life. Some copy precisely, others generally. Some can learn from recorded songs, others need live tutors. Some use their fathers as tutors, others use neighbors. These stylistic variations in song learning reflect differences among species in their social systems and histories, with each style being honed by specific ecological circumstances.

Songs Convey Information

When a bird sings, it produces a signal that conveys information to receivers, for example, from males competing for territories to females choosing mates. Behavioral ecologists have determined that song deters territorial intrusions by competitors and that complex songs and large repertoires deter rivals more effectively than simple songs or small repertoires. Males with complex songs and large repertoires also pair earlier, obtain more mates, and produce more offspring. When females choose mates, song indicates some aspect of male quality, from good genes to strong parenting abilities.

When the interests of the sender and receiver conflict, such as when males compete for territories or females choose mates, songs tend to be loud and conspicuous. Conflict often yields an evolutionary "arms race" between senders trying to manipulate receivers with their signals and receivers warily assessing signals for quality and reliability. Songs tend to be quiet and inconspicuous, however, when the shared information is mutually beneficial—when songbirds elicit alarm calls warning others of an approaching raptor, for example.

Song learning may help songbirds adapt to their social environment, it may promote the formation of new species, or it may ensure that birds' songs transmit well through the habitat in which they are sung. Still, there are many unanswered questions and there is much to explore about how and why birds sing.

Yellow-billed Magpie   {*Pica nuttalli*}

DATE   LOCATION

American Crow   {*Corvus brachyrhynchos*}

DATE   LOCATION

Northwestern Crow   {*Corvus caurinus*}

DATE   LOCATION

Mexican Crow   {*Corvus imparatus*}

DATE   LOCATION

Fish Crow   {*Corvus ossifragus*}

DATE   LOCATION

Chihuahuan Raven   {*Corvus cryptoleucus*}

DATE   LOCATION

Common Raven   {*Corvus corax*}

DATE   LOCATION

Titmice   {Family Paridae}

Black-capped Chickadee   {*Parus atricapillus*}

DATE   LOCATION

Carolina Chickadee

{*Parus carolinensis*}

DATE

LOCATION

Mountain Chickadee

{*Parus gambeli*}

DATE

LOCATION

Siberian Tit

{*Parus cinctus*}

DATE

LOCATION

Boreal Chickadee

{*Parus hudsonicus*}

DATE

LOCATION

Chestnut-backed Chickadee

{*Parus rufescens*}

DATE

LOCATION

Bridled Titmouse

{*Parus wollweberi*}

DATE

LOCATION

Plain Titmouse

{*Parus inornatus*}

DATE

LOCATION

Tufted Titmouse

{*Parus bicolor*}

DATE *April, 2003*

LOCATION *Noblesville, IN Back yard (not first)*

Verdins   {Family Remizidae}

....

Verdin   {*Auriparus flaviceps*}

DATE   LOCATION

Bushtits   {Family Aegithalidae}

....

Bushtit   {*Psaltriparus minimus*}

DATE   LOCATION

Nuthatches   {Family Sittidae}

....

Red-breasted Nuthatch   {*Sitta canadensis*}

DATE frequent   LOCATION Noblesville, IN, 1185 N. 19th &
                                                 White River Trail

....

White-breasted Nuthatch   {*Sitta carolinensis*}

DATE   LOCATION

Nuthatches *(cont'd)*   {Family Sittidae}

Pygmy Nuthatch   {*Sitta pygmaea*}

DATE   LOCATION

Brown-headed Nuthatch   {*Sitta pusilla*}

DATE   LOCATION

Creepers   {Family Certhiidae}

Brown Creeper   {*Certhia americana*}

DATE   LOCATION

Bulbuls   {Family Pycnonotidae}

Red-whiskered Bulbul   {*Pycnonotus jocosus*}

DATE   LOCATION

Cactus Wren

{*Campylorhynchus brunneicapillus*}

DATE

LOCATION

Rock Wren

{*Salpinctes obsoletus*}

DATE

LOCATION

Canyon Wren

{*Catherpes mexicanus*}

DATE

LOCATION

Carolina Wren

{*Thryothorus ludovicianus*}

DATE

LOCATION

Wrens *(cont'd)*   {Family Troglodytidae}

Bewick's Wren   { *Thryomanes bewickii* }

DATE   LOCATION

House Wren   { *Troglodytes aedon* }

DATE   LOCATION

Winter Wren   { *Troglodytes troglodytes* }

DATE   LOCATION

Sedge Wren   { *Cistothorus platensis* }

DATE   LOCATION

Marsh Wren

DATE

{*Cistothorus palustris*}

LOCATION

Dippers

{Family Cinclidae}

American Dipper

DATE

{*Cinclus mexicanus*}

LOCATION

Old World Warblers and Thrushes

{Family Muscicapidae}

Arctic Warbler

DATE

{*Phylloscopus borealis*}

LOCATION

Golden-crowned Kinglet

DATE

{*Regulus satrapa*}

LOCATION

Ruby-crowned Kinglet   {*Regulus calendula*}

DATE   LOCATION

Blue-gray Gnatcatcher   {*Polioptila caerulea*}

DATE 4-16-2003   LOCATION Muscatatuck NWR, Jackson Co, IN

California Gnatcatcher   {*Polioptila californica*}

DATE   LOCATION

Black-tailed Gnatcatcher   {*Polioptila melanura*}

DATE   LOCATION

WINTER IN VERMONT

1.

*F*ive
jays
discuss
goodandevil
in a
white
birch

like five
blue
fingers
playing
a
guitar.

2.

Snow bunting whirling
on a snowy field—
cutglass reflections
on a ceiling.

3.

Lover of balsam and lover of white pine
o crossbill crossbill
cracking unseen with of all things scissors
seeds seeds
a fidget for ears enpomped in the meadow's
silence silence
a crackling thorn aflame in the meadow's
cold cold.

4.

Small things
    are hardest to believe:
a redpoll snatching
    drops from an icicle.

5.

The song of the gray
ninepointed buck
contains much contains
the whole north for
example the sweet
sharp whistling of
the redpolls caught
overhead in the branches
of the yellow birch
like leaves left over
from autumn and at
night the remote
chiming of stars
caught in the tines
of his quiet exaltation.

HAYDEN CARRUTH

Black-capped Gnatcatcher

{ *Polioptila nigriceps* }

DATE   LOCATION

Bluethroat

{ *Luscinia svecica* }

DATE   LOCATION

Northern Wheatear

{ *Oenanthe oenanthe* }

DATE   LOCATION

Eastern Bluebird

{ *Sialia sialis* }

DATE   LOCATION

Western Bluebird {*Sialia mexicana*}

DATE

LOCATION

Mountain Bluebird {*Sialia currucoides*}

DATE

LOCATION

Townsend's Solitaire {*Myadestes townsendi*}

DATE

LOCATION

Veery {*Catharus fuscescens*}

DATE

LOCATION

Within a thick and spreading hawthorn bush
That overhung a molehill large and round,
I heard from morn to morn a merry thrush
Sing hymns to sunrise, and I drank the sound
With joy;

from THE THRUSH'S NEST
John Clare

Gray-cheeked Thrush　　　　　{ *Catharus minimus* }

DATE　　　　　LOCATION

Bicknell's Thrush　　　　　{ *Catharus bicknelli* }

DATE　　　　　LOCATION

Swainson's Thrush　　　　　{ *Catharus ustulatus* }

DATE　　　　　LOCATION

Hermit Thrush　　　　　{ *Catharus guttatus* }

DATE　　　　　LOCATION

Wood Thrush   {Hylocichla mustelina}

DATE   LOCATION

Clay-colored Robin   {Turdus grayi}

DATE   LOCATION

A bird came down the walk:
He did not know I saw;
He bit an angleworm in halves
And ate the fellow raw.

American Robin   {Turdus migratorius}

DATE   LOCATION

from A BIRD CAME DOWN THE WALK
Emily Dickinson

Varied Thrush   {Ixoreus naevius}

DATE   LOCATION

Old World Warblers and Thrushes *(cont'd)* {Family Muscicapidae}

Wrentit

{*Chamaea fasciata*}

DATE

LOCATION

Mimic-Thrushes {Family Mimidae}

Gray Catbird

{*Dumetella carolinensis*}

DATE

LOCATION

Northern Mockingbird

{*Mimus polyglottos*}

DATE

LOCATION

Sage Thrasher

{*Oreoscoptes montanus*}

DATE

LOCATION

Migration

IN NORTH AMERICA about two-thirds of all species migrate at least several hundred miles from summer nesting habitats to wintering grounds. Of these, at least one hundred species head for the tropical climates of the Caribbean and Central and South America. Migration to warmer climates occurs because of decreasing amounts of food and fewer hours of feeding time per day in northern latitudes. Birds, such as swallows and flycatchers, that feed on flying insects for a large part of their diet have two options: migrate or hibernate. In North America, only the Common Poorwill, a small relative of the nightjar group, goes into hibernation. Migration is the overwhelming choice.

The migratory journey is a necessary but perilous one. Birds leave their familiar nesting habitats, exposing themselves to such deadly weather extremes as hailstorms and hurricanes. They often fly over inhospitable regions—large lakes, bays, and oceans—where they find neither shelter nor food and are vulnerable to predators such as hawks and owls. And after surviving all the unknowns in transit, they must compete with resident birds for food.

HOMECOMING

It may seem strange that northern migrants don't choose to stay in the balmy south rather than repeat the hazardous return trip the following spring, but tropical climates are not as benevolent as they appear. Food is often scarce. The soil is often low in nutrients, and warm temperatures increase the rate of decomposition, which results in rapid nutrient recycling and keen pressure among plants and insects to avoid being consumed. In contrast, northern soils are comparatively rich in such nutrients as calcium and phosphorus. When the spring thaw finally occurs, northern forests and wetlands provide an enormous flush of protein to migrant birds. Melting ice and warming temperatures provide ideal conditions for

More than three million Snow Geese leave the far north for the winter.

mosquitoes, blackflies, midges, and other tiny invertebrates, and the arrival of insect-eating migratory birds coincides perfectly with the hatches of these flying insects. An abundance of bugs permits most migrants to lay larger clutches of eggs than their nonmigratory tropical relatives and to raise more young. Migrants can also raise more broods in the north because the days are longer and chicks can receive more food.

THE MECHANICS

Migration southward and spring return are mainly linked to daylight, which stimulates the production of hormones that drive the migratory urge. (Local weather may also affect the "travel itinerary," because many birds wait for favorable tailwinds to assist them over long flights.) Day length determines spring arrival dates, which are often remarkably constant—Arctic Terns, for example, which nest on Matinicus Rock in Maine, return from wintering grounds in Antarctica with extraordinary punctuality, usually settling into traditional nesting places on May 13.

Using star patterns, most small land birds travel at night. By flying during the cooler hours, they can conserve water, thereby reducing the number of stops necessary for refueling and drinking—and the chance of attacks by predators.

A radar study of fall migrants flying over Cape Cod, Massachusetts, found that most birds fly about 1,500 to 2,500 feet above ground early in the evening, but at 5,000 to 9,000 feet later at night. Thrushes may fly at heights of 3.5 miles, songbirds at just under one mile. The speed of the trips varies seasonally, with northbound migrants in the spring in a much greater rush to secure quality nesting territories than those heading south in the fall. The robin is a relatively slow traveler, averaging about thirty-seven miles a day, while the tiny Blackpoll Warbler may travel two hundred miles daily on the home stretch from South America to northern Canada. With the aid of a powerful tailwind, migrating waterfowl and shorebirds may travel up to one thousand miles nonstop in twenty-four hours.

NAVIGATION

Each fall, millions of parent shorebirds and songbirds head south, leaving their offspring to find their way to ancestral wintering grounds on their own. Geese, swans, and cranes migrate south as family units, but such parental escorts for the young are the exception rather than the rule. The specific navigation methods that migrants use to find their way between nesting and wintering habitats are little known, but most have a variety of skills that they apply to different circumstances. On clear nights, birds may follow star patterns, particularly the North Star and

Arctic Tern,
by John James Audubon

associated circumpolar constellations, but in cases of overcast skies, they may rely on magnetic fields. (Studies of homing pigeons have revealed millions of tiny magnetic grains positioned in the front of the bird's brain, which help them detect subtle changes in the earth's magnetic field.) Birds may also refer to visual landmarks, the position of the sun, distant sounds, and even smells. Birds have very accurate "biological clocks" that aid them in knowing how long to migrate in a particular direction.

EFFECTS OF URBANIZATION

Migration, always a high-risk proposition, is further compromised by mazes of tall buildings and communication towers that sparkle enticingly. And many of the key feeding habitats for coastal migrants have been transformed into sterile suburbs where millions of birds crash against windows and fall prey to family cats. Cerulean Warbler and Wood Thrush populations are declining because of habitat loss in the northeastern United States and in the tropics. Fragmentation—the cutting up of forests by roads, power lines, and suburbanization—gives nest and egg predators, such as grackles and jays, access to forest interiors and makes nests vulnerable to kleptoparasitic Brown-headed Cowbirds, which slip their own eggs into the nests of other species.

Brown Pelicans are "partial migrants." Northern populations move away from their colonies post-breeding season.

Mimic-Thrushes (cont'd)   {Family Mimidae}

Brown Thrasher   {*Toxostoma rufum*}

DATE   LOCATION

Long-billed Thrasher   {*Toxostoma longirostre*}

DATE   LOCATION

Bendire's Thrasher   {*Toxostoma bendirei*}

DATE   LOCATION

Curve-billed Thrasher   {*Toxostoma curvirostre*}

DATE   LOCATION

Mimic-Thrushes (cont'd)   {Family Mimidae}

California Thrasher   {*Toxostoma redivivum*}

DATE   LOCATION

Crissal Thrasher   {*Toxostoma crissale*}

DATE   LOCATION

Le Conte's Thrasher   {*Toxostoma lecontei*}

DATE   LOCATION

Wagtails and Pipits   {Family Motacillidae}

Yellow Wagtail   {*Motacilla flava*}

DATE   LOCATION

White Wagtail   {Motacilla alba}

DATE   LOCATION

Black-backed Wagtail   {Motacilla lugens}

DATE   LOCATION

Red-throated Pipit   {Anthus cervinus}

DATE   LOCATION

American Pipit   {Anthus rubescens}

DATE   LOCATION

| Wagtails and Pipits | {Family Motacillidae} |

Sprague's Pipit
{Anthus spragueii}

DATE

LOCATION

| Waxwings | {Family Bombycillidae} |

Bohemian Waxwing
{Bombycilla garrulus}

DATE

LOCATION

Cedar Waxwing
{Bombycilla cedrorum}

DATE

LOCATION

| Silky-Flycatchers | {Family Ptilogonatidae} |

Phainopepla
{Phainopepla nitens}

DATE

LOCATION

Shrikes {Family Laniidae}

Northern Shrike {*Lanius excubitor*}

DATE LOCATION

Loggerhead Shrike {*Lanius ludovicianus*}

DATE LOCATION

Starlings {Family Sturnidae}

European Starling {*Sturnus vulgaris*}

DATE LOCATION

Crested Myna {*Acridotheres cristatellus*}

DATE LOCATION

Hill Myna   {*Gracula religiosa*}

DATE   LOCATION

Vireos   {Family Vireonidae}

White-eyed Vireo   {*Vireo griseus*}

DATE   LOCATION

Bell's Vireo   {*Vireo bellii*}

DATE   LOCATION

Black-capped Vireo   {*Vireo atricapillus*}

DATE   LOCATION

Gray Vireo   { *Vireo vicinior* }

DATE   LOCATION

Solitary Vireo   { *Vireo solitarius* }

DATE   LOCATION

Yellow-throated Vireo   { *Vireo flavifrons* }

DATE   LOCATION

Hutton's Vireo   { *Vireo huttoni* }

DATE   LOCATION

Warbling Vireo

{ *Vireo gilvus* }

DATE   LOCATION

Philadelphia Vireo

{ *Vireo philadelphicus* }

DATE   LOCATION

Red-eyed Vireo

{ *Vireo olivaceus* }

DATE   LOCATION

Black-whiskered Vireo

{ *Vireo altiloquus* }

DATE   LOCATION

WARBLERS
Wood Warblers

{Family Emberizidae}
{Subfamily Parulinae}

Blue-winged Warbler

{*Vermivora pinus*}

DATE

LOCATION

Golden-winged Warbler

{*Vermivora chrysoptera*}

DATE

LOCATION

Tennessee Warbler

{*Vermivora peregrina*}

DATE

LOCATION

Orange-crowned Warbler

{*Vermivora celata*}

DATE

LOCATION

Nashville Warbler {*Vermivora ruficapilla*}

DATE   LOCATION

Virginia's Warbler {*Vermivora virginiae*}

DATE   LOCATION

Colima Warbler {*Vermivora crissalis*}

DATE   LOCATION

Lucy's Warbler {*Vermivora luciae*}

DATE   LOCATION

Northern Parula

DATE

{ *Parula americana* }

LOCATION

Tropical Parula

DATE

{ *Parula pitiayumi* }

LOCATION

Yellow Warbler

DATE

{ *Dendroica petechia* }

LOCATION

Chestnut-sided Warbler

DATE

{ *Dendroica pensylvanica* }

LOCATION

Magnolia Warbler {*Dendroica magnolia*}

DATE LOCATION

Cape May Warbler {*Dendroica tigrina*}

DATE LOCATION

Black-throated Blue Warbler {*Dendroica caerulescens*}

DATE LOCATION

Yellow-rumped Warbler {*Dendroica coronata*}

DATE LOCATION

Black-throated Gray Warbler

{ *Dendroica nigrescens* }

DATE

LOCATION

Townsend's Warbler

{ *Dendroica townsendi* }

DATE

LOCATION

Hermit Warbler

{ *Dendroica occidentalis* }

DATE

LOCATION

Black-throated Green Warbler

{ *Dendroica virens* }

DATE

LOCATION

Golden-cheeked Warbler   {*Dendroica chrysoparia*}

DATE   LOCATION

Blackburnian Warbler   {*Dendroica fusca*}

DATE   LOCATION

Yellow-throated Warbler   {*Dendroica dominica*}

DATE   LOCATION

Grace's Warbler   {*Dendroica graciae*}

DATE   LOCATION

Pine Warbler   {*Dendroica pinus*}

DATE   LOCATION

Kirtland's Warbler   {*Dendroica kirtlandii*}

DATE   LOCATION

Prairie Warbler   {*Dendroica discolor*}

DATE   LOCATION

Palm Warbler   {*Dendroica palmarum*}

DATE   LOCATION

Bay-breasted Warbler   {*Dendroica castanea*}

DATE   LOCATION

Blackpoll Warbler   {*Dendroica striata*}

DATE   LOCATION

Cerulean Warbler   {*Dendroica cerulea*}

DATE   LOCATION

Black-and-white Warbler   {*Mniotilta varia*}

DATE   LOCATION

The Nocturnal World

AS SOON as the last light fades, the last robin's song dies away, and the last swift swirls into its chimney to roost, a new world awakens—the world of nighttime birds and animals.

It begins with a sound: The persistent *peent* of a woodcock readying its crepuscular mating display. The strident call of a Common Nighthawk overhead as it snags insects. The distinctive whistles, both musical and oddly mechanical, that give the Whip-poor-will, Chuck-will's-widow, and Common Poorwill their names. The various clicks, ticks, and peeps of the rails, birds of the marshes. The fabulous, wild yodeling of loons. And, deep in the night, the throaty hooting and mysterious wails of those most emblematic of nocturnal birds, the owls.

Keen senses are the currency of the nighttime world. Owls locate their prey with a combination of highly sensitive hearing and exceptional eyesight. Closely related to the owls are the Nightjars—the family of birds that includes Whip-poor-wills, Chuck-will's-widows, Nighthawks, and their kin. Nightjars—the name refers to the abrasive sound of their nocturnal calls—are also known as "goatsuckers" (the literal translation of their Latin name *Caprimulgus*), from an ancient Greek belief that these birds came in the night to steal milk from their goat herds. One South American Nightjar species, the Oilbird, finds its way in the dark by using echolocation—the same technique employed by bats.

Contrary to popular conceptions, however, most sharp-visioned nightjars need some light to hunt their prey (moths and other insects). And they do not, as was once believed, "vacuum" bugs from the air with their large mouths. Whip-poor-wills hunt by moonlight and can recognize their favorite prey items. They are even thought to synchronize the rearing of their young to the full moon, to get the best hunting when they need

Red-winged Blackbird at dusk

it the most. Nighthawks do not really fly by darkest night, and are most active at dawn and dusk.

The strangest of all nocturnal birds, the flightless Kiwi of New Zealand, relies on a highly developed sense of smell. It is the only bird to have its nostrils situated at the end of its long curved bill. Kiwis sometimes give away their presence by emitting a "snuffling" or "snorting" sound as they smell for worms, grubs, and other food along the ground.

Because the hearing of many nocturnal birds is extremely sensitive, silence is also highly valued at night, especially among predators. Incredibly soft, specially constructed flight feathers (the primary feather on the leading edge of each wing is serrated, eliminating the sound of air flowing over it) allow them to swoop silently through the skies.

The calls of many owls, rails, and nightjars are remarkably resonant, allowing them to communicate over great distances to find mates and defend territories. Nighthawks have in their repertoire a resounding *swoosh*, produced by air rushing over the male's wings as he dives to impress an amorous female or to ward off a competitor.

For sheer weirdness in night sounds, however, another New Zealand specialty takes the prize. The Kakapo, an extremely rare, flightless, nocturnal parrot, gives a nighttime mating performance second to none. The male digs out a circular area of bare ground, known as a lek, where he stages his show. As night falls, he begins emitting a hollow "booming" noise, produced by inflating air sacs in his chest. The sound is sometimes likened to rolling thunder, and is audible from up to several miles away on a calm night. The calling lasts all night, or until a female arrives on the lek. When she does, the male throws in a little dance for good measure, and then the mating proceeds.

THE ENIGMATICAL OWL

The owl has been a symbolic figure for centuries, and its elusiveness sustains its mythology. It has been equated with power, wisdom, and royalty, and appears frequently on ancient Egyptian hieroglyphs.

Owls have amazing hearing and eyesight. An owl's round, concave facial structure acts like a parabolic dish to magnify minute sounds. Enhancing this natural "amplifier" are the openings of an owl's ears; asymmetrically situated, one high and one low, they allow the bird to "triangulate" its prey, locating it, just by sound, to within inches. The owl's extraordinary eyes do the rest. (They are nearly as large as human eyes but are considered at least one hundred times more sensitive and are equipped with many sensitive rods for excellent night vision.)

THE LATE SHIFT

It's unclear why certain birds have evolved to become part of the nightlife. For owls, nighttime is when many of their favorite prey become active. Nightjars, too, find the nocturnal world a feast of moths and other insects. Nighttime frees these birds from competition with other species that prey upon their resources during the day, and may also make them less obvious to diurnal predators. A majority of

Black Rail
by John James Audubon

owls and nightjars spend the daytime roosting and usually have elaborate cryptic coloration—camouflage that makes them nearly invisible to the human eye.

Whatever their reason, these are not the only feathered denizens of the nocturnal world. It is also occasionally inhabited by many birds commonly considered to be daytime species, such as warblers, vireos, thrushes, and other songbirds. During the spring and fall migrations, when these birds travel up to several thousand miles between breeding and wintering grounds, the bulk of their journey takes place at night. Often flying nonstop until dawn, navigating by a combination of the stars, the Earth's electromagnetic field, and other cues, these birds flap steadily through the night and ride the winds to save energy, while also avoiding the threat of hungry daytime predators such as hawks and falcons.

Great Horned Owl

In a few cases, the reverse is true, and residents of the night world make use of daylight: Nighthawks, for example, become active diurnally during migrations, when they gather in flocks to feed on the wing before heading on their way.

It is an old birder's tradition to count the passage of migrants silhouetted against a full moon. Recently, a brilliant young scientist at the Cornell Laboratory of Ornithology, Bill Evans, devised a method of recording and identifying night migrants' calls, resulting in new insights into the phenomenon of migration.

Today, the myths and mysteries of nocturnal birds are beginning to fall away as ornithologists learn more about avian habits and lifestyles. But a deep fascination with these creatures will never completely disappear. To know the birds of the night is to inhabit a world in which senses are heightened, making the thrill of discovery and recognition even more precious.

American Redstart {*Setophaga ruticilla*}

DATE

LOCATION

Prothonotary Warbler {*Protonotaria citrea*}

DATE

LOCATION

Worm-eating Warbler {*Helmitheros vermivorus*}

DATE

LOCATION

Swainson's Warbler {*Limnothlypis swainsonii*}

DATE

LOCATION

Ovenbird {*Seiurus aurocapillus*}

DATE LOCATION

Northern Waterthrush {*Seiurus noveboracensis*}

DATE LOCATION

Louisiana Waterthrush {*Seiurus motacilla*}

DATE LOCATION

Kentucky Warbler {*Oporornis formosus*}

DATE LOCATION

Connecticut Warbler {*Oporornis agilis*}

DATE   LOCATION

Mourning Warbler {*Oporornis philadelphia*}

DATE   LOCATION

MacGillivray's Warbler {*Oporornis tolmiei*}

DATE   LOCATION

Common Yellowthroat {*Geothlypis trichas*}

DATE   LOCATION

Wood Warblers *(cont'd)*   {Subfamily Parulinae}

Hooded Warbler   {*Wilsonia citrina*}

DATE   LOCATION

Wilson's Warbler   {*Wilsonia pusilla*}

DATE   LOCATION

Canada Warbler   {*Wilsonia canadensis*}

DATE   LOCATION

Red-faced Warbler   {*Cardellina rubrifrons*}

DATE   LOCATION

Tanagers   {Subfamily Thrampinae}

Painted Redstart   {*Myioborus pictus*}

DATE   LOCATION

Yellow-breasted Chat   {*Icteria virens*}

DATE   LOCATION

Hepatic Tanager   {*Piranga flava*}

DATE   LOCATION

Summer Tanager   {*Piranga rubra*}

DATE   LOCATION

Tanagers (cont'd) {Subfamily Thraupinae}

Scarlet Tanager {*Piranga olivacea*}

DATE LOCATION

Western Tanager {*Piranga ludoviciana*}

DATE LOCATION

Flame-colored Tanager {*Piranga bidentata*}

DATE LOCATION

Cardinals {Subfamily Cardinalinae}

Northern Cardinal {*Cardinalis cardinalis*}

DATE LOCATION

Pyrrhuloxia   {Cardinalis sinuatus}

DATE   LOCATION

Rose-breasted Grosbeak   {Pheucticus ludovicianus}

DATE   LOCATION

Black-headed Grosbeak   {Pheucticus melanocephalus}

DATE   LOCATION

Blue Grosbeak   {Guiraca caerulea}

DATE   LOCATION

Cardinals *(cont'd)*   {Subfamily Cardinalinae}

Lazuli Bunting   {*Passerina amoena*}

DATE   LOCATION

Indigo Bunting   {*Passerina cyanea*}

DATE   LOCATION

Varied Bunting   {*Passerina versicolor*}

DATE   LOCATION

Painted Bunting   {*Passerina ciris*}

DATE   LOCATION

Dickcissel   {Spiza americana}

DATE   LOCATION

New World Sparrows   {Subfamily Emberizinae}

Olive Sparrow   {Arremonops rufivirgatus}

DATE   LOCATION

Green-tailed Towhee   {Pipilo chlorurus}

DATE   LOCATION

Spotted Towhee   {Pipilo maculatus}

DATE   LOCATION

Eastern Towhee

{*Pipilo erythrophthalmus*}

DATE   LOCATION

California Towhee

{*Pipilo crissalis*}

DATE   LOCATION

Canyon Towhee

{*Pipilo fuscus*}

DATE   LOCATION

Albert's Towhee

{*Pipilo aberti*}

DATE   LOCATION

Bachman's Sparrow   {*Aimophila aestivalis*}

DATE   LOCATION

Botteri's Sparrow   {*Aimophila botterii*}

DATE   LOCATION

Cassin's Sparrow   {*Aimophila cassinii*}

DATE   LOCATION

Rufous-winged Sparrow   {*Aimophila carpalis*}

DATE   LOCATION

Rufous-crowned Sparrow {*Aimophila ruficeps*}

DATE LOCATION

American Tree Sparrow {*Spizella arborea*}

DATE LOCATION

Chipping Sparrow {*Spizella passerina*}

DATE LOCATION

Clay-colored Sparrow {*Spizella pallida*}

DATE LOCATION

Brewer's Sparrow {*Spizella breweri*}

DATE

LOCATION

Field Sparrow {*Spizella pusilla*}

DATE

LOCATION

Black-chinned Sparrow {*Spizella atrogularis*}

DATE

LOCATION

Vesper Sparrow {*Pooecetes gramineus*}

DATE

LOCATION

The first sparrow of spring! The year beginning with younger hope than ever! The faint silvery warblings heard over the partially bare and moist fields from the bluebirds, the song sparrow, and the redwing, as if the last flakes of winter tinkled as they fell! What at such times are histories, chronologies, traditions, and all written revelations?

"SPRING" FROM *WALDEN*
Henry David Thoreau

Lark Sparrow   {Chondestes grammacus}

DATE   LOCATION

Black-throated Sparrow   {Amphispiza bilineata}

DATE   LOCATION

Sage Sparrow   {Amphispiza belli}

DATE   LOCATION

Five-striped Sparrow   {Amphispiza quinquestriata}

DATE   LOCATION

Lark Bunting   {Calamospiza melanocorys}

DATE   LOCATION

Savannah Sparrow   {Passerculus sandwichensis}

DATE   LOCATION

Baird's Sparrow   {Ammodramus bairdii}

DATE   LOCATION

Grasshopper Sparrow   {Ammodramus savannarum}

DATE   LOCATION

Henslow's Sparrow {Ammodramus henslowii}

DATE   LOCATION

Le Conte's Sparrow {Ammodramus leconteii}

DATE   LOCATION

Saltmarsh Sharp-tailed Sparrow {Ammodramus caudacutus}

DATE   LOCATION

Nelson's Sharp-tailed Sparrow {Ammodramus nelsoni}

DATE   LOCATION

The Bird in Art

THROUGHOUT HISTORY, the beauty of birds has always inspired artists. Think of the splendid plumage of the Bird of Paradise, Peacock, and Scarlet Macaw, of the snow-white dove and bluebird, of gliding flight, strutting courtship dances and displays.

Early peoples, fascinated and awed by these creatures, carved images out of stone, wood, and bone, and painted them on the walls of caves (France's Lescaux and Trois Frères are the most famous examples). Feathered masks, capes, and head-dresses were worn in ceremonies in Africa, South and North America, and the Pacific islands in the belief that the wearer would be endowed with the character-istics of the bird, as well as attain its power to approach the gods and to carry divine messages for hunting, healing, and solving problems.

The ancient Egyptians considered their artwork not only representations of the deities but also containers of the deities' sacred energy, forces for good and evil in themselves. They believed their king was an incarnation of the sky god, Horus, who appeared as a falcon, often depicted with clearly rendered heads and feet and more generalized bodies and wings. Swallows, whose migratory patterns were interpreted as a sign of regeneration, were frequently carved in votives.

Wheatfield with Crows (1890), *by Vincent van Gogh*

In Classical Greece, sculpted birds were included in the friezes on the pediments of temples. Birds were also painted on numerous vases in a style that makes them look rounded, not flat. Hunting scenes and stories about the gods and goddesses are frequently the subjects.

In Asian cultures, birds, especially the crane and heron, became early symbols of peace and tranquillity. The crane became a symbol of immortality, fidelity, and vigilance to the Chinese. In India the peacock's wheel-like iridescent tail symbolized the sun in all its glory, the starry heavens, and the unity of the cosmos. Hindu inconography represents the bird as the mount of Kama, the god of love, and the sacred animal of Saravati, goddess of wisdom and poetry.

Celebration of Spirit

Starting in the Middle Ages, birds became prominent in the paintings, sculpture, and architecture honoring Christianity. From the exquisite illuminated manuscripts of the ninth and tenth centuries to the splendid paintings depicting the Old and New Testaments over the next several centuries, doves appear as symbols of the Holy Spirit.

In fourteenth-century Europe, art became more humanistic—Giotto's painting of St. Francis preaching to the birds is a fine example. The Renaissance, freed from restrictive canons, led to a luxuriant flower-

Tree with Birds (1996), *by Aaron Birnbaum*

ing of art and produced some of the world's greatest artists: Raphael, Michelangelo, Botticelli, Da Vinci.

By the twentieth century, art had largely freed iself from religious traditions and turned to the secular and personal. Vincent van Gogh's *Wheatfield with Crows,* painted the day before his suicide in 1890, is an intensely dramatic depiction of a flock of black crows, traditional harbingers of death, flying over a shimmering sun-drenched field. Picasso's *Guernica* (1937), a three-hundred-foot memorial to the Spanish victims of a Nazi massacre, is presided over by a shrieking dove of peace. And sculptor Constantin Brancusi used steel chrome, the popular new medium in a world of machinery, to fashion his Bird in Space, an abstract creature in flight, sleek and smooth, without feathers or other details to distract one's touch.

GALLERY OF ARTISTS

The tradition of illustrating birds on printed plates in ornithological books began in Europe as early as the fifteenth century. In 1555, Pierre Belon published a *History of the Nature of Birds,* with 160 woodcuts, in Paris. In the eighteenth century, the Count de Buffon's *Natural History of Animals* contained 1,000 plates of birds. Others

Landscape with swallow, detail of Aegean fresco (c. 1650 BCE)

followed, laying the foundation for the most famous of all—John James Audubon. A self-trained artist, he probed the secrets of fields, woods, and swamps to place his intricately painted birds in appropriate settings, producing four volumes of plates between 1827 and 1838.

There have been other noteworthies in the gallery of bird artists. John Gould (1804–1881), Audubon's English rival, became the most prolific European bird illustrator of the nineteenth century. Edward Lear (1812–1888) collaborated with Gould on several of his major works. Scotsman Archibald Thorburn (1860–1935) illustrated the seminal ornithological four-volume work *British Birds*, which today is better known for its plates than its text. George Edward Lodge (1860–1953), skilled in oil painting, was considered peerless when it came to painting birds of prey.

White Heron Landing Behind Irises
(c. 1830), *by Ando Hiroshige*

Bruno Liljefors (1860–1939), a Swede, is recognized as the father of modern wildlife painting. Louis Agassiz Fuertes (1874–1927) was one of the world's finest bird portraitists; Roger Tory Peterson (1908–1996), for whom the field guide plate was an art form that demanded discipline and organization, combined a flawless technique with a keen eye of naturalistic detail.

Robert Bateman (b. 1930) is one of the finest modern-day wildlife artists, whose birds are technically superlative. Guy Tudor (b. 1936) beautifully translates soft feathers into solid shapes; John P. O'Neill (b. 1942) is acclaimed as one of the foremost painters of tropical birds. Lars Johnson (b. 1952) is a Swedish-born artist often compared to the old masters Liljefors, Thorburn, and Fuertes.

Today, artistically rendered birds are present in our everyday life in pottery, jewelry, textiles, and photography. Whatever the medium, these images of birds are as comforting and delightful to us as birds themselves.

New World Sparrows *(cont'd)*   {Subfamily Emberizinae}

Seaside Sparrow   {*Ammodramus maritimus*}

DATE   LOCATION

Fox Sparrow   {*Passerella iliaca*}

DATE   LOCATION

Song Sparrow   {*Melospiza melodia*}

DATE   LOCATION

Lincoln's Sparrow   {*Melospiza lincolnii*}

DATE   LOCATION

Swamp Sparrow {Melospiza georgiana}

DATE   LOCATION

White-throated Sparrow {Zonotrichia albicollis}

DATE 4- 16-2003   LOCATION Muscatatuck NWR, Seymour, Jackson Co, I.

Golden-crowned Sparrow {Zonotrichia atricapilla}

DATE 4-16-2003   LOCATION Muscatatuck NWR, Seymour, Jackson Co, IN

White-crowned Sparrow {Zonotrichia leucophrys}

DATE 4 - 16 - 2003   LOCATION Muscatatuck NWR, Seymour, Jackson Co IN

Harris's Sparrow   {Zonotrichia querula}

DATE   LOCATION

Dark-eyed Junco   {Junco hyemalis}

DATE   LOCATION

Yellow-eyed Junco   {Junco phaeonotus}

DATE   LOCATION

McCown's Longspur   {Calcarius mccownii}

DATE   LOCATION

New World Sparrows *(cont'd)*   {Subfamily Emberizinae}

Lapland Longspur

{*Calcarius lapponicus*}

DATE   LOCATION

Smith's Longspur

{*Calcarius pictus*}

DATE   LOCATION

Chestnut-collared Longspur

{*Calcarius ornatus*}

DATE   LOCATION

Snow Bunting

{*Plectrophenax nivalis*}

DATE   LOCATION

In Act III, Scene V, of Shakespeare's *The Tragedy of Romeo and Juliet,* the two star-crossed lovers meet in the Capulets' orchard. It is the first time they have spoken since Romeo went into hiding following his deadly clash with Tybalt, Juliet's cousin.

Enter Romeo and Juliet aloft [at the window].

Juliet: Wilt thou be gone? It is not yet near day.
It was the nightingale, and not the lark,
That pierc'd the fearful hollow of thine ear.
Nightly she sings on yond pomegranate tree.
Believe me, love, it was the nightingale.

Romeo: It was the lark, the herald of the morn;
No nightingale. Look, love, what envious streaks
Do lace the severing clouds in yonder East.
Night's candles are burnt out, and jocund day
Stands tiptoe on the misty mountain tops.
I must be gone and live, or stay and die.

Juliet: Yond light is not daylight; I know it, I.
It is some meteor that the sun exhales
To be to thee this night a torchbearer
And light thee on the way to Mantua.
Therefore stay yet; thou need'st not to be gone.

Romeo: Let me be ta'en, let me be put to death.
I am content, so thou wilt have it so.
I'll say yon grey is not the morning's eye,
'Tis but the pale reflex of Cynthia's brow;
Nor that is not the lark whose notes do beat
The vaulty heaven so high above our heads.
I have more care to stay than will to go.
Come, death, and welcome! Juliet wills it so.
How is't, my soul? Let's talk; it is not day.

Juliet: It is, it is! Hie hence, be gone, away!
It is the lark that sings so out of tune,
Straining harsh discords and unpleasing sharps.
Some say the lark makes sweet division;
This doth not so, for she divideth us.
Some say the lark and loathed toad chang'd eyes;
O, now I would they had chang'd voices too,
Since arm from arm that voice doth us affray,
Hunting thee hence with hunt's-up to the day!
O, now be gone! More light and light it grows.

Romeo: More light and light—more dark and dark
our woes!

New World Sparrows *(cont'd)*   {Subfamily Emberizinae}

McKay's Bunting

{Plectrophenax hyperboreus}

DATE   LOCATION

New World Blackbirds and Orioles   {Subfamily Icterinae}

Bobolink

{Dolichonyx oryzivorus}

DATE   LOCATION

Red-winged Blackbird

{Agelaius phoeniceus}

DATE   LOCATION

Tricolored Blackbird

{Agelaius tricolor}

DATE   LOCATION

Eastern Meadowlark

DATE

{ *Sturnella magna* }

LOCATION

Western Meadowlark

DATE

{ *Sturnella neglecta* }

LOCATION

Yellow-headed Blackbird

DATE

{ *Xanthocephalus xanthocephalus* }

LOCATION

Rusty Blackbird

DATE

{ *Euphagus carolinus* }

LOCATION

Brewer's Blackbird

{ *Euphagus cyanocephalus* }

DATE

LOCATION

Great-tailed Grackle

{ *Quiscalus mexicanus* }

DATE

LOCATION

Boat-tailed Grackle

{ *Quiscalus major* }

DATE

LOCATION

Common Grackle

{ *Quiscalus quiscula* }

DATE

LOCATION

Shiny Cowbird

{ _Molothrus bonariensis_ }

DATE   LOCATION

Bronzed Cowbird

{ _Molothrus aeneus_ }

DATE   LOCATION

Brown-headed Cowbird

{ _Molothrus ater_ }

DATE   LOCATION

Orchard Oriole

{ _Icterus spurius_ }

DATE   LOCATION

Hooded Oriole   {*Icterus cucullatus*}

DATE   LOCATION

Spot-breasted Oriole   {*Icterus pectoralis*}

DATE   LOCATION

Altamira Oriole   {*Icterus gularis*}

DATE   LOCATION

Audubon's Oriole   {*Icterus graduacauda*}

DATE   LOCATION

How is't each bough a several music yields?
The lusty throstle, early nightingale,
Accord in tune, though vary in their tale;
The chirping swallow call'd forth by the sun,
And crested lark doth his divisions run?
The yellow bees the air with murmur fill,
The finches carol, and the turtles bill?
Whose power is this? what god?

NATURE'S ACCORD
Ben Jonson

Baltimore Oriole

{ *Icterus galbula* }

DATE

LOCATION

Bullock's Oriole

{ *Icterus bullockii* }

DATE

LOCATION

Scott's Oriole

{ *Icterus parisorum* }

DATE

LOCATION

Finches

{Family Fringillidae}

Brambling

{ *Fringilla montifringilla* }

DATE

LOCATION

Gray-crowned Rosy-Finch   {*Leucosticte tephrocotis*}

DATE   LOCATION

Black Rosy-Finch   {*Leucosticte atrata*}

DATE   LOCATION

Brown-capped Rosy-Finch   {*Leucosticte australis*}

DATE   LOCATION

Pine Grosbeak   {*Pinicola enucleator*}

DATE   LOCATION

Purple Finch   {Carpodacus purpureus}

DATE   LOCATION

Cassin's Finch   {Carpodacus cassinii}

DATE   LOCATION

House Finch   {Carpodacus mexicanus}

DATE   LOCATION

Red Crossbill   {Loxia curvirostra}

DATE   LOCATION

White-winged Crossbill   {*Loxia leucoptera*}

DATE   LOCATION

Common Redpoll   {*Carduelis flammea*}

DATE   LOCATION

Hoary Redpoll   {*Carduelis hornemanni*}

DATE   LOCATION

Pine Siskin   {*Carduelis pinus*}

DATE   LOCATION

Lesser Goldfinch

DATE

{ *Carduelis psaltria* }

LOCATION

Lawrence's Goldfinch

DATE

{ *Carduelis lawrencei* }

LOCATION

American Goldfinch

DATE

{ *Carduelis tristis* }

LOCATION

European Goldfinch

DATE

{ *Carduelis carduelis* }

LOCATION

Evening Grosbeak   {*Coccothraustes vespertinus*}

DATE   LOCATION

Old World Sparrows   {Family Passeridae}

House Sparrow   {*Passer domesticus*}

DATE   LOCATION

Eurasian Tree Sparrow   {*Passer montanus*}

DATE   LOCATION

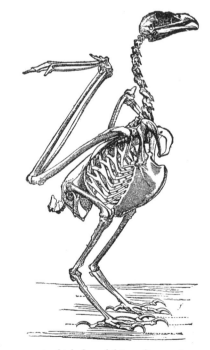

Are birds descended from dinosaurs?

The Dinosaur Debate

THE AUGUST 1996 discovery of an apparent "feathered dinosaur" fossil rekindled a long-running debate about the origin of birds. On one side of the controversy stand dinosaur paleontologists who are persuaded, because of a mass of fossil evidence, that birds are the direct descendants of dinosaurs. Aligned on the opposite side are many ornithologists who openly scoff at the bird-dinosaur link, arguing that the paleontologists may know dinosaur fossils but understand little about birds.

The "feathered dinosaur" fossil, believed to be at least 120 million years old, was found by a local fossil hunter in China's Liaoning province, an area rich in dinosaur and ancient bird remains. A slab of mudstone, split into two pieces, contained the unmistakable petrified remains of a small two-legged dinosaur with a row of featherlike appendages running from its head to its tail. For Philip Currie, dinosaur curator of the Royal Tyrell Museum of Palaeontology in Alberta, Canada, there was only one possible reaction: "What I saw was breathtaking. It was a feathered dinosaur." Alan Feducci, an ornithologist at the University of North Carolina at Chapel Hill, disagreed. "I've studied enlarged photos of that thing, and I'll tell you this, those aren't feathers."

An international group of paleontologists went to China to study the new fossil and announced its findings in April 1997. Because the scientists had only three days to examine the fossil, they reached no firm conclusions, but they did agree that under a microscope the dark-colored ridges did not resemble feathers. One member of the group, though, postulated

Marabou Stork

that modern feathers could have evolved from this dinosaur's ridged appendages, or that the appendages might be a different type of feather altogether. These findings only added fuel to the bird-dinosaur debate, and pointed to the need for continued research.

POINT COUNTERPOINT

The bird-dinosaur debate originated in 1868 when British biologist Thomas H. Huxley proposed that two fossils discovered in a German quarry seven years earlier established a link between birds and dinosaurs. One, a crow-sized creature named *Archaeopteryx* and dated to 150 million years ago, was the earliest fossilized bird ever discovered. The other, a new dinosaur dubbed *Composgnathus,* had long, delicate hind limbs and a foot and ankle joint almost indistinguishable from that of a bird. "It is impossible to look at the conformation of this strange reptile," Huxley asserted, "and to doubt that it hopped or walked . . . after the manner of a bird."

For more than fifty years, the bird-dinosaur link was widely accepted, but in 1926, Danish paleontologist Gerhard Heilman rejected the connection, noting that dinosaurs, particularly the small bipedal ones that looked most birdlike, lacked a key avian feature: the clavicles, or collarbones, that in birds developed into the wishbone. Heilman thought it was wiser to look for birds' ancestors in the earlier reptiles, and proposed that the archosaurs, dating to about 230 million years ago, were the ancestors that gave rise to dinosaurs, pterosaurs (flying reptiles), crocodilians, and birds. This theory did not completely sever the bird-dinosaur tie because it stated that birds are as related to dinosaurs as they are crocodilians and pterosaurs.

Heilman's theory held sway for much of the twentieth century. In 1973, however, Yale University paleontologist John Ostrom revived Huxley's idea, arguing forcefully that *Archaeopteryx* was a dinosaur, noting that it had features virtually indistinguishable from the two-legged dinosaurs known collectively as "theropods." Most significant, new dinosaur specimens discovered in the Gobi Desert and in Montana had clavicles. Over the next two decades, as more and more theropod fossils were found, the bird-dinosaur link became tighter, with the 1996 discovery in China being the latest and potentially most signficant.

Most paleontologists remain convinced that birds are dinosaurs. Among the key characteristics common to both are the three-toed foot, crescent-shaped carpal bone in the wrist, orientation of the pubic bones, bipedal stance, and wishbone. Paleontologist Paul Sereno has noted, "Everywhere we look, from their skeletal fea-

A trio of intriguingly equipped Roseate Spoonbills

tures to their behaviors to even the microstructure of their eggs, we see evidence that birds are descended from dinosaurs."

Ornithologists argue that many of the similarities between birds and dinosaurs are merely the result of parallel evolution. Feducci has used the example of flightless birds, such as ostriches and emus, that have evolved on different continents. "They look alike because of their mode of life, not because they both descended from a common ancestor." He has also pointed out that the bird-dinosaur group does not have an adequate explanation for how birds began to fly. He scoffs at their notion that small dinosaurs mastered flight by running along the ground and leaping into the air. "Any engineer will tell you that's aerodynamically impossible," Feducci has asserted.

Perhaps the most pointed issue in the debate is timing. The first bird, *Archaeopteryx*, dates to the late Jurassic period, 150 million years ago, but the earliest dinosaurs that paleontologists have tried to link with birds didn't appear until 30 million years later. While the bird-dinosaur group has few doubts that their theory will be vindicated when the fossils of *Archaeopteryx*'s ancestors—small, swift theropod dinosaurs—are found, some ornithologists believe the fossils of creatures that produced the avian line will prove to be lightly built, tree-dwelling reptiles.

These arguments have led many scientists—including ornithologist Frank B. Gill, director of science at the National Audubon Society—to agree that the bird-dinosaur link requires closer scrutiny. "I used to be into the dinosaur origin of birds hook, line, and sinker," says Dr. Gill. "But I'm not anymore; I think there are different ways to interpret the fossil record, and both sides should be listened to." And so, both sides eagerly await new discoveries that they hope will settle the bird-dinosaur debate once and for all.

Sinosauropteryx prima

American Birding Association's Principles of Birding Ethics

EVERYONE WHO ENJOYS BIRDS AND BIRDING must always respect wildlife, its environment, and the rights of others. In any conflict of interest between birds and birders, the welfare of the birds and their environment comes first.

CODE OF BIRDING ETHICS

1. Promote the welfare of birds and their environment.

1(a). Support the protection of important bird habitat.

1(b). To avoid stressing birds or exposing them to danger, exercise restraint and caution during observation, photography, sound recording, or filming.

Limit the use of recordings and other methods of attracting birds, and never use such methods in heavily birded areas, or for attracting any species that is Threatened, Endangered, or of Special Concern, or is rare in your local area.

Keep well back from nests and nesting colonies, roosts, display areas, and important feeding sites. In such sensitive areas, if there is a need for extended observation, photography, filming, or recording, try to use a blind or hide, and take advantage of natural cover.

Use artificial light sparingly for filming or photography, especially for close-ups.

1(c). Before advertising the presence of a rare bird, evaluate the potential for disturbance to the bird, its surroundings, and other people in the area, and proceed only if access can be controlled, disturbance minimized, and permission has been obtained from private land-owners. The sites of rare nesting birds should be divulged only to the proper conservation authorities.

1(d). Stay on roads, trails, and paths where they exist; otherwise keep habitat disturbance to a minimum.

2. Respect the law, and the rights of others.

2(a). Do not enter private property without the owner's explicit permission.

2(b). Follow all laws, rules, and regulations governing use of roads and public areas, both at home and abroad.

2(c). Practice common courtesy in contacts with other people. Your exemplary behavior will generate goodwill with birders and non-birders alike.

3. Ensure that feeders, nest structures, and other artificial bird environments are safe.

3(a). Keep dispensers, water, and food clean, and free of decay or disease. It is important to feed birds continually during harsh weather.

3(b). Maintain and clean nest structures regularly.

3(c). If you are attracting birds to an area, ensure the birds are not exposed to predation from cats and other domestic animals, or dangers posed by artificial hazards.

4. Group birding, whether organized or impromptu, requires special care.

Each individual in the group, in addition to the obligations spelled out in Items #1 and #2, has responsibilities as a Group Member.

4(a). Respect the interests, rights, and skills of fellow birders, as well as people participating in other legitimate outdoor activities. Freely share your knowledge and experience, except where code I(c) applies. Be especially helpful to beginning birders.

4(b). If you witness unethical birding behavior, assess the situation, and intervene if you think it prudent. When interceding, inform the person(s) of the inappropriate action, and attempt, within reason, to have it stopped. If the behavior continues, document it, and notify appropriate individuals or organizations.

Group Leader Responsibilities [amateur and professional trips and tours].

4(c). Be an exemplary ethical role model for the group. Teach through word and example.

4(d). Keep groups to a size that limits impact on the environment, and does not interfere with others using the same area.

4(e). Ensure everyone in the group knows of and practices this code.

4(f). Learn and inform the group of any special circumstances applicable to the areas being visited (e.g., no tape recorders allowed).

4(g). Acknowledge that professional tour companies bear a special responsibility to place the welfare of birds and the benefits of public knowledge ahead of the company's commercial interests. Ideally, leaders should keep track of tour sightings, document unusual occurrences, and submit records to appropriate organizations.

Please follow this code and distribute and teach it to others.

ABOUT NATIONAL AUDUBON SOCIETY

AT NATIONAL AUDUBON SOCIETY our mission is to protect the wildlife and wildlife habitat upon which our lives depend. Together with more than 550,000 members and an extensive chapter network, our professional staff of scientists, lobbyists, lawyers, policy analysts, and educators is fighting to save threatened ecosystems and to restore the natural balance that is critical to the quality of life on our planet. Our underlying belief is that all forms of life are interdependent and that the diversity of nature is essential to both our economic and environmental well-being.

CHAPTERS

Audubon's 550,000 members provide the underpinning for all the society's programs and activities. Three-fourths of our members also belong to local Audubon chapters, now numbering more than five hundred, which serve in their communities as focal points for conservation, nature education, and citizen action on environmental issues.

SANCTUARIES

Through its nationwide system of sanctuaries, Audubon protects more than 150,000 acres of essential habitat and unique natural areas for birds, other wild animals, and rare plants. The sanctuaries range in size from two and one half acres of tidal flats in Washington's Nisqually River Delta to twenty-six hundred acres of coastal marsh in Louisiana. Most are staffed by resident managers and wardens, who also protect the larger natural systems in which the sanctuaries exist. Many are sites for new Audubon centers, places on the land where people gather to interact with nature and other nature lovers, to grow in their commitment to protecting the Earth.

STATE FIELD OFFICES

We have an expanding network of state offices that spearheads Audubon's conservation and education programs throughout the fifty states. In partnership with Audubon chapter volunteers, field staff are advancing the creation of "a culture of conservation in communities throughout America." This includes activities ranging from establishing Audubon nature centers to identifying and conserving important bird areas. They conduct citizen leadership training workshops to build awareness and participation in the environmental policy process at every level of government.

PUBLIC POLICY

Audubon provides advocacy for national and regional campaigns through our Washington, D.C., office. Staff meet with federal agencies, testify before Congress, and pursue environmental litigation where appropriate. We also cooperate with other conservation organizations on local and national issues.

SCIENCE

Science steers conservation at Audubon; citizens provide the power. Together, we successfully drive conservation action at every level—community, state, national, and international. Audubon Science uncovers the problems and points to solutions, helping to guide all of Audubon, from education to policy. Three major programs—Watchlist, Important Bird Areas, and Birdsource—form the foundation of bird conservation at Audubon. Our Living Oceans program protects vital fish stocks and marine habitats, and our Seabird Restoration program successfully reestablishes bird colonies.

PUBLICATION

Our award-winning *Audubon* magazine, published six times a year, carries outstanding articles and color photography on wildlife and nature. It presents in-depth reports on critical environmental issues, as well as conservation news and comment. Audubon is sent to all members and, by subscription, to thousands of libraries, schools, and government agencies. The Audubon Books division develops books and electronic products with various publishing houses and partners. With twenty million copies in print, National Audubon Society field guides are recognized as essential reference tools for understanding the natural world.

EDUCATION

Audubon Adventures, a four-page children's newspaper, reaches five hundred thousand elementary students in fifteen thousand classrooms nationwide. Audubon also operates education centers throughout the country. There, teacher-naturalists hold outdoor classes for schoolchildren and other groups, as well as provide outreach and teacher training at local schools and parks. Our summer ecology camps—in Maine, Vermont, Minnesota, Connecticut, and Wyoming—provide intensive study sessions for adults, youths, and families and carry optional university credit. Audubon Expedition Institute offers undergraduate and graduate degree environmental studies programs in the United States for college students and special sessions for advanced-level high school students.

TRAVEL

National Audubon Society Nature Odysseys sponsors nature-oriented travel programs worldwide to destinations including Africa, Alaska, Antarctica, Baja California, Costa Rica, Galápagos, and locations across the United States. All tour operators must comply with our Travel Ethic for Environmentally Responsible Travel, and each trip is led by an experienced Audubon senior staff member. For information contact National Audubon Society Nature Odysseys, 700 Broadway, New York, NY 10003; or call (212) 979-3066; or E-mail: travel@audubon.org.

TELEVISION

Created in 1984, Audubon Productions has maintained its original commitment to providing quality entertainment that educates and informs people about the environment. Audubon Productions has produced more than forty "World of Audubon" Specials for Turner Broadcasting System (TBS), a series of natural history programs entitled *"Audubon's Animal Adventures"* for the Disney Channel, and various other videos and interactive products that seek to raise environmental awareness.

NATIONAL AUDUBON SOCIETY HEADQUARTERS AND FIELD OFFICES

Visit our website @ http://www.audubon.org

NATIONAL HEADQUARTERS
700 Broadway • New York, NY 10003–9562
(212) 979-3000

PUBLIC POLICY
1901 Pennsylvania Avenue, NW, Suite 1100
Washington, DC 20006
(202) 861-2242

NATIONAL FIELD OFFICE
(Guam, Puerto Rico, and states not covered by a state office)
555 Audubon Place • Sacramento, CA 95825
(916) 481-5332

LATIN AMERICA AND CARIBBEAN PROGRAM
444 Brickell Avenue, Suite 850 • Miami, FL 33131
(305) 371-6399

ALASKA STATE OFFICE
308 G Street, Suite 217 • Anchorage, AL 99501
(907) 276-7034

CALIFORNIA STATE OFFICE (also serves NV)
555 Audubon Place • Sacramento, CA 95825
(916) 481-5332

AUDUBON CENTER IN GREENWICH
(serves Connecticut as a state office)
613 Riverville Road • Greenwich, CT 06831
(203) 869-5272

COLORADO STATE OFFICE
3109 28th Street
Boulder, CO 80301
(303) 415-0130

FIELD SUPPORT OFFICE
(AZ, DE, ID, OK, DC)
3109 28th Street • Boulder, CO 80301
(303) 415-0130

FLORIDA AUDUBON SOCIETY
1331 Palmetto Avenue, Suite 110 • Winter Park, FL 32789
(407) 539-5700

IOWA STATE OFFICE
P.O. Box 71174 • Des Moines, IA 50325
(515) 267-0701

MAINE STATE REPRESENTATIVE
P.O. Box 524 • Dover-Foxcroft, ME 04426
(207) 564-7946

MINNESOTA STATE OFFICE
26 East Exchange Street, Suite 207 • St. Paul, MN 55101
(612) 225-1830

MISSISSIPPI STATE OFFICE (also serves AL)
285 East Falconer Street • Holly Spring, MS 38635
(601) 252-4143

MONTANA AUDUBON
324 Fuller Avenue • P.O. Box 595 • Helena, MT 59624
(406) 443-3949

NEBRASKA AUDUBON
P.O. Box 117
Denton, NE 68339
(402) 797-2301

NEW MEXICO STATE OFFICE
Randall Davey Audubon Center
P.O. Box 9314 • Santa Fe, NM 87504–9314
(505) 983-4609

NEW YORK STATE OFFICE
200 Trillium Lane • Albany, NY 12203
(518) 869-9731

NORTH CAROLINA STATE OFFICE
720 Market Street • Wilmington, NC 28401
(910) 251-0666

NORTH DAKOTA STATE OFFICE
Black Building • 118 Broadway, Suite 502 • Fargo, ND 58102
(701) 298-3373

OHIO STATE OFFICE
692 N. High Street, Suite 208 • Columbus, OH 43215
(614) 224-1585

PENNSYLVANIA STATE OFFICE
1104 Fernwood Avenue, Suite 300 • Camp Hill, PA 17011
(717) 763-4985

SOUTH CAROLINA STATE OFFICE
336 Sanctuary Road
Harleysville, SC 29448
(843) 462-2160

TEXAS STATE OFFICE
2525 Wallingwood, Suite 301 • Austin, TX 78746
(512) 306-0225

UTAH STATE OFFICE
549 Cortez
Salt Lake City, UT 84103
(801) 355-8110

VERMONT STATE OFFICE
65 Millet Street • P.O. Box 5 • Richmond, VT 05477
(802) 434-4300

WASHINGTON STATE OFFICE
P.O. Box 462 • Olympia, WA 98507
(360) 786-8020

WYOMING AUDUBON
101 Garden Creek Road
Casper, WY 82604
(307) 235-3485

EDUCATION CENTERS AND OFFICES

NATIONAL AUDUBON SOCIETY EDUCATION DIVISION
700 Broadway • New York, NY 10003–9562
(212) 979-3183

AUDUBON CENTER IN GREENWICH
613 Riversville Road • Greenwich, CT 06831
(203) 869-5272

AUDUBON EXPEDITION INSTITUTE
P.O. Box 365 • Belfast, ME 04915
(207) 338-5859

AULLWOOD AUDUBON CENTER AND FARM
1000 Aullwood Road • Dayton, OH 45414
(937) 890-7360

BENT OF THE RIVER AUDUBON CENTER
185 East Flat Hill Road • Southbury, CT 06488
(203) 264-5098

LOS ANGELES EDUCATION CENTER
National Audubon Society
6042 Monte Vista Street • Los Angeles, CA 90042
(323) 254-0252

PICKERING CREEK ENVIRONMENTAL CENTER
11450 Audubon Lane
Easton, MD 21601
(410) 822-4903

RANDALL DAVEY AUDUBON CENTER
P.O. Box 9314 • Santa Fe, NM 87504
(505) 983-2880

RICHARDSON BAY AUDUBON CENTER
AND SANCTUARY
376 Greenwood Beach Road • Tiburon, CA 94920
(415) 388-2524

SCHLITZ AUDUBON CENTER
1111 East Brown Deer Road • Milwaukee, WI 53217
(414) 352-2880

SHARON AUDUBON CENTER
325 Cornwall Bridge Road • Sharon, CT 06069
(860) 364-0520

WILDLIFE SANCTUARIES

Sanctuaries marked with an asterisk have limited visitation. You must make arrangements in advance.

NATIONAL FIELD OFFICE
555 Audubon Place • Sacramento, CA 95825
(916) 481-5332

FRANCIS BEIDLER FOREST SANCTUARY
336 Sanctuary Road • Harleyville, SC 29448
(843) 462-2150/2160

BORESTONE MOUNTAIN WILDLIFE SANCTUARY
P.O. Box 524 • Dover-Foxcroft, ME 04426
(207) 631-4050 (summer)
(207) 564-7946 (winter)

CLYDE E. BUCKLEY WILDLIFE SANCTUARY
1305 Germany Road • Frankfort, KY 40601
(606) 873-5711

CONSTITUTION MARSH SANCTUARY
P.O. Box 174 • Cold Spring, NY 10516
(914) 265-2601

CORKSCREW SWAMP SANCTUARY
375 Sanctuary Road West • Naples, FL 34120
(941) 348-9151

NORTH CAROLINA COASTAL ISLANDS SANCTUARY*
720 Market Street • Wilmington, NC 28401
(910) 762-9534

PINE ISLAND SANCTUARY*
P.O. Box 174 • Poplar Branch, NC 27965
(252) 453-2838

LILLIAN ANNETTE ROWE SANCTUARY*
Route 2, P.O. Box 146 • Gibbon, NE 68840
(308) 468-5282

SABAL PALM GROVE
P.O. Box 5052 • Brownsville, TX 78523
(956) 541-8034

SCIENCE AND FIELD RESEARCH OFFICES

NATIONAL AUDUBON SOCIETY
Science Division Headquarters
700 Broadway • New York, NY 10003–9562
(212) 979-3000

SCULLY SCIENCE CENTER
550 South Bay Avenue • Islip, NY 11751
(516) 859-3032

SEABIRD RESTORATION PROGRAM
AND PUFFIN PROJECT
159 Sapsucker Woods Road • Ithaca, NY 14850
(207) 529-5828 (summer)
(607) 257-7308 (winter)

BIRDING AND CONSERVATION ORGANIZATIONS
AND GOVERNMENT AGENCIES

AMERICAN BIRDING ASSOCIATION
P.O. Box 6599 • Colorado Springs, CO 80934
(800) 850-2473
http://www.americanbirding.org

AMERICAN ORNITHOLOGISTS' UNION
c/o Division of Birds MRC 116
National Museum of Natural History • Washington, DC 20560
(202) 357-2051
http://www.nmnh.si.edu/BIRDNET/AOU

CANADIAN NATURE FEDERATION
1 Nicholas Street, Suite 606 • Ottawa, Ontario K1N 7B7
(613) 562-3447
http://www.cnf.cal

CORNELL LABORATORY OF ORNITHOLOGY
159 Sapsucker Woods Road • Ithaca, NY 14851
(607) 254-2440
http://www.ornith.cornell.edu

ENVIRONMENT CANADA
351 St. Joseph Boulevard • Hull, Quebec K1A OH3
(819) 997-1095
http://www.cciw.ca/green-lane/wildlife

NATIONAL AUDUBON SOCIETY
700 Broadway • New York, NY 10003
(212) 979-3000
http://www.audubon.org

NATIONAL GEOGRAPHIC SOCIETY
1145 17th Street, NW • Washington, DC 20036
(888) 647-6733
http://www.nationalgeographic.com

NATIONAL WILDLIFE FEDERATION
8925 Leesburg Pike • Vienna, VA 22184
(703) 790-4100
http://www.nwf.org

THE NATURE CONSERVANCY
4245 North Fairfax Drive • Arlington, VA 22203
(703) 841-5300
http://www.tnc.org

SIERRA CLUB
85 Second Street • San Francisco, CA 94105–3441
(415) 977-5500
http://www.sierraclub.com

U.S. FISH AND WILDLIFE SERVICE
Department of the Interior
1849 C Street, NW • Washington, DC 20240
(202) 208-5634
http://www.fws.gov

WILSON ORNITHOLOGICAL SOCIETY
University of Michigan
Museum of Zoology
1109 Geddes Avenue • Ann Arbor, MI 48109–1079
(734) 764-0457
http://www.ummz.lsa.umich.edu/birds/wos.html

WORLD WILDLIFE FUND
1250 24th Street, NW • Washington, DC 20037
(202) 293-4800
http://www.wwf.org

BUILDING A BASIC BIRD LIBRARY

THESE ARE SOME RECOMMENDED TITLES that should roost on every bird lover's bookshelf:

Field guides are indispensable tools for the precise identification of bird species. No one guide, however, fulfiills every need, so most birders find themselves buying several different guides. Among the most useful field guides are Roger Tory Peterson's classic *Peterson's Field Guide: Eastern Birds* (Boston: Houghton Mifflin, 1980) and *Peterson's Field Guide: Western Birds* (Boston: Houghton Mifflin, 1990); *National Audubon Society Field Guide to North American Birds: Eastern Region,* by John Bull and John Farrand Jr. (New York: Knopf, 1994) and *National Audubon Society Field Guide to North American Birds: Western Region,* by Miklos D. F. Udvardy and John Farrand Jr. (New York: Knopf, 1997), which both feature superb photographs; and Chandler S. Robbins's easy-to-use *Birds of North America* (New York: Golden Press, 1983). It's also vital for bird lovers to own books that focus on the birds in their area. To determine which regional bird books are the best for you, ask the nearest Audubon Society chapter.

Experienced birders will want a copy of the *National Geographic Society's Field Guide to the Birds of North America,* ed., Shirley L. Scott (Washington, D.C.: National Geographic Society, 1993). Kenn Kaufman's *Field Guide to Advanced Birding* (Boston: Houghton Mifflin, 1990) is an excellent choice for experts. Kaufman's *Lives of North American Birds* (Boston: Houghton Mifflin, 1996) and John Terres's *The Audubon Society's Encyclopedia of North American Birds* (New York: Knopf, 1987) are outstanding references for those who want to know more about birds than what field guides provide.

Frank B. Gill's *Ornithology* (New York: Freeman, 1994) provides thorough and astute coverage of bird biology. Of the many titles on bird behavior, A. F. Skutch's *Parent Birds and Their Young* (Austin: University of Texas Press, 1976) and Paul J. Baicich's and Colin James Oliver Harrison's *A Guide to the Nests, Eggs and Nestlings of North American Birds* (New York: Academic Press, 1997) are standouts.

For those keen on attracting birds to their backyards, Robert Burton's *National Audubon Society North American Birdfeeder Handbook* (New York: Dorling Kindersley, 1995), Stephen W. Kress's *National Audubon Society The Bird Garden* (New York: Dorling Kindersley, 1995), and John Terres's and Roger Tory Peterson's *Songbirds in Your Garden* (Chapel Hill, N.C.: Algonquin, 1994) are excellent choices.

For more titles, you should consult John Terres's *The Audubon Society's Encyclopedia of North American Birds,* which contains an excellent selected reading list and an extensive bibliography that will point you to leading bird books.

PUBLICATIONS

AUDUBON
c/o National Audubon Society
700 Broadway • New York, NY 10003–9562
(212) 979-3000
http://magazine.audubon.org
e-mail: editor@audubon.org

BIRDER'S WORLD
21027 Crossroads Circle • Waukesha, WI 53186
(414) 796-8776
http://www.kalmbach.com/birders/world.html

BIRDING
P.O. Box 6599 • Colorado Springs, CO 80934
(800) 850-2473
http://www.americanbirding.org/bdggen.htm
e-mail: member@aba.org

THE BIRDS OF NORTH AMERICA
P.O. Box 1897 • Lawrence, KS 66044
(800) 627-0629
http://www.birdsofna.org
e-mail: tammyb@allenpress.com

BIRD WATCHER'S DIGEST
P.O. Box 110 • Marietta, OH 45750
(740) 373-5285
http://www.petersononline.com/birds/bwd/index.html
e-mail: ReadBWD@aol.com

FIELD NOTES
c/o American Birding Association
P.O. Box 6599 • Colorado Springs, CO 80934
(800) 850-2473
http://www.americanbirding.org/fldngen.htm
e-mail: member@aba.org

WILD BIRD
Fancy Publications, Inc.
P.O. Box 6050 • Mission Viejo, CA 92690
(714) 855-8822

LIFE-LIST CHECKLIST INDEX

☐ Lesser Scaup (*Aythya affinis*)

☐ Common Eider (*Somateria mollissima*)   43

☐ King Eider (*Somateria spectabilis*)

☐ Spectacled Eider (*Somateria fischeri*)

☐ Steller's Eider (*Polysticta stelleri*)

☐ Harlequin Duck (*Histrionicus histrionicus*)   44

☐ Oldsquaw (*Clangula hyemalis*)

☐ Black Scoter (*Melanitta nigra*)

☐ Surf Scoter (*Melanitta perspicillata*)

☐ White-winged Scoter (*Melanitta fusca*)   45

☐ Common Goldeneye (*Bucephala clangula*)

☐ Barrow's Goldeneye (*Bucephala islandica*)

☐ Bufflehead (*Bucephala albeola*)

☐ Hooded Merganser (*Lophodytes cucullatus*)   46

☐ Common Merganser (*Mergus merganser*)

☐ Red-breasted Merganser (*Mergus serrator*)

☐ Ruddy Duck (*Oxyura jamaicensis*)

☐ Masked Duck (*Oxyura dominica*)   47

NEW WORLD VULTURES, HAWKS AND EAGLES,
    AND FALCONS (*Order Falconiformes*)   47

☐ Black Vulture (*Coragyps atratus*)

☐ Turkey Vulture (*Cathartes aura*)

☐ California Condor (*Gymnogyps californianus*)

☑ Osprey (*Pandion haliaetus*)   48

☐ Hook-billed Kite (*Chondrohierax uncinatus*)

☐ Swallow-tailed Kite (*Elanoides forficatus*)

☐ White-tailed Kite (*Elanus leucurus*)

☑ Snail Kite (*Rostrhamus sociabilis*)   49

☐ Mississippi Kite (*Ictinia mississippiensis*)

☐ Bald Eagle (*Haliaeetus leucocephalus*)

☐ Northern Harrier (*Circus cyaneus*)

☐ Sharp-shinned Hawk (*Accipiter striatus*)   50

☐ Cooper's Hawk (*Accipiter cooperii*)

☐ Northern Goshawk (*Accipiter gentilis*)

☐ Common Black-Hawk (*Buteogallus anthracinus*)

☐ Harris's Hawk (*Parabuteo unicinctus*)   51

☐ Gray Hawk (*Buteo nitidus*)

☐ Red-shouldered Hawk (*Buteo lineatus*)

☑ Broad-winged Hawk (*Buteo platypterus*)

☐ Short-tailed Hawk (*Buteo brachyurus*)   52

☐ Swainson's Hawk (*Buteo swainsoni*)

☐ White-tailed Hawk (*Buteo albicaudatus*)

☐ Zone-tailed Hawk (*Buteo albonotatus*)

☑ Red-tailed Hawk (*Buteo jamaicensis*)   53

☐ Ferruginous Hawk (*Buteo regalis*)

☐ Rough-legged Hawk (*Buteo lagopus*)

☐ Golden Eagle (*Aquila chrysaetos*)

☐ Crested Caracara (*Caracara plancus*)   54

☐ American Kestrel (*Falco sparverius*)

☐ Merlin (*Falco columbarius*)

☐ Aplomado Falcon (*Falco femoralis*)

☐ Peregrine Falcon (*Falco peregrinus*)   55

☐ Gyrfalcon (*Falco rusticolus*)

☐ Prairie Falcon (*Falco mexicanus*)

PHEASANTS, GROUSE, AND QUAILS
    (*Order Galliformes*)   55

☐ Gray Partridge (*Perdix perdix*)

☐ Chukar (*Alectoris chukar*)   56

☐ Ring-necked Pheasant (*Phasianus colchicus*)

☐ Spruce Grouse (*Dendragapus canadensis*)

☐ Blue Grouse (*Dendragapus obscurus*)

☐ Willow Ptarmigan (*Lagopus lagopus*)   61

☐ Rock Ptarmigan (*Lagopus mutus*)

☐ White-tailed Ptarmigan (*Lagopus leucurus*)

☐ Ruffed Grouse (*Bonasa umbellus*)

☐ Sage Grouse (*Centrocercus urophasianus*)   62

☐ Greater Prairie-chicken (*Tympanuchus cupido*)

☐ Lesser Prairie-chicken
    (*Tympanuchus pallidicinctus*)

☐ Sharp-tailed Grouse
    (*Tympanuchus phasianellus*)

☐ Wild Turkey (*Meleagris gallopavo*)   63

☐ Montezuma Quail (*Cyrtonyx montezumae*)

☐ Northern Bobwhite (*Colinus virginianus*)

☐ Scaled Quail (*Callipepla squamata*)

☐ Gambel's Quail (*Callipepla gambelii*)   66

☐ California Quail (*Callipepla californica*)

☐ Mountain Quail (*Oreortyx pictus*)

RAILS, COOTS, LIMPKINS, AND CRANES
    (*Order Gruiformes*)   66

☐ Yellow Rail (*Coturnicops noveboracensis*)

☐ Black Rail (*Laterallus jamaicensis*)   67

☐ Clapper Rail (*Rallus longirostris*)

☐ King Rail (*Rallus elegans*)

☐ Virginia Rail (*Rallus limicola*)

☐ Sora (*Porzana carolina*)   68

☐ Purple Gallinule (*Porphyrula martinica*)

☐ Common Moorhen (*Gallinula chloropus*)

☑ American Coot (*Fulica americana*)

☐ Limpkin (*Aramus guarauna*)   69

☐ Sandhill Crane (*Grus canadensis*)

☑ Whooping Crane (*Grus americana*)

SHOREBIRDS, WADERS, GULLS, AND DIVING
    BIRDS (*Order Charadriiformes*)   69

PLOVERS, OYSTERCATCHERS, STILTS, AND
    AVOCETS (*Suborder Charadrii*)

☐ Northern Lapwing (*Vanellus vanellus*)

☐ Black-bellied Plover (*Pluvialis squatarola*)   70

☐ American Golden-Plover
    (*Pluvialis dominicus*)

☐ Pacific Golden-Plover (*Pluvialis fulva*)

☐ Snowy Plover (*Charadrius alexandrinus*)

☐ Wilson's Plover (*Charadrius wilsonia*)   71

☐ Semipalmated Plover
    (*Charadrius semipalmatus*)

☐ Piping Plover (*Charadrius melodus*)

☑ Killdeer (*Charadrius vociferus*)

☐ Mountain Plover (*Charadrius montanus*)   72

☐ American Oystercatcher
    (*Haematopus palliatus*)

☐ Black Oystercatcher (*Haematopus bachmani*)

☐ Black-necked Stilt (*Himantopus mexicanus*)

☐ American Avocet (*Recurvirostra americana*)   73

JACANAS AND SANDPIPERS (*Suborder Scolopaci*)   73

☐ Northern Jacana (*Jacana spinosa*)

☐ Greater Yellowlegs (*Tringa melanoleuca*)

☐ Lesser Yellowlegs (*Tringa flavipes*)

☐ Solitary Sandpiper (*Tringa solitaria*)   74

☐ Willet (*Catoptrophorus semipalmatus*)

☐ Wandering Tattler (*Heteroscelus incanus*)

☐ Gray-tailed Tattler (*Heteroscelus brevipes*)

☐ Spotted Sandpiper (*Actitis macularia*)   75

☐ Upland Sandpiper (*Bartramia longicauda*)

☐ Whimbrel (*Numenius phaeopus*)

☐ Bristle-thighed Curlew (*Numenius tahitiensis*)

☐ Long-billed Curlew (*Numenius americanus*)   76

☐ Black-tailed Godwit (*Limosa limosa*)

☐ Hudsonian Godwit (*Limosa haemastica*)

☐ Bar-tailed Godwit (*Limosa lapponica*)
☐ Marbled Godwit (*Limosa fedoa*)   81
☐ Ruddy Turnstone (*Arenaria interpres*)
☐ Black Turnstone (*Arenaria melanocephala*)
☐ Surfbird (*Aphriza virgata*)
☐ Red Knot (*Calidris canutus*)   82
☐ Sanderling (*Calidris alba*)
☐ Semipalmated Sandpiper (*Calidris pusilla*)
☐ Western Sandpiper (*Calidris mauri*)
☐ Least Sandpiper (*Calidris minutilla*)   83
☐ White-rumped Sandpiper (*Calidris fuscicollis*)
☐ Baird's Sandpiper (*Calidris bairdii*)
☐ Pectoral Sandpiper (*Calidris melanotos*)
☐ Sharp-tailed Sandpiper (*Calidris acuminata*)   84
☐ Purple Sandpiper (*Calidris maritima*)
☐ Rock Sandpiper (*Calidris ptilocnemis*)
☐ Dunlin (*Calidris alpina*)
☐ Curlew Sandpiper (*Calidris ferruginea*)   85
☐ Stilt Sandpiper (*Calidris himantopus*)
☐ Buff-breasted Sandpiper (*Tryngites subruficollis*)
☐ Ruff (*Philomachus pugnax*)
☐ Short-billed Dowitcher (*Limnodromus griseus*) 86
☐ Long-billed Dowitcher
     (*Limnodromus scolopaceus*)
☐ Common Snipe (*Gallinago gallinago*)
☐ American Woodcock (*Scolopax minor*)
☐ Wilson's Phalarope (*Phalaropus tricolor*)   87
☐ Red-necked Phalarope (*Phalaropus lobatus*)
☐ Red Phalarope (*Phalaropus fulicaria*)

GULLS, TERNS, AND SKIMMERS (*Suborder Lari*)   87
☐ Pomarine Jaeger (*Stercorarius pomarinus*)
☐ Parasitic Jaeger (*Stercorarius parasiticus*)   88
☐ Long-tailed Jaeger (*Stercorarius longicaudus*)
☐ Laughing Gull (*Larus atricilla*)
☐ Franklin's Gull (*Larus pipixcan*)
☐ Little Gull (*Larus minutus*)   89
☐ Black-headed Gull (*Larus ridibundus*)
☐ Bonaparte's Gull (*Larus philadelphia*)
☐ Heermann's Gull (*Larus heermanni*)
☐ Mew Gull (*Larus canus*)   90
☐ Ring-billed Gull (*Larus delawarensis*)
☐ California Gull (*Larus californicus*)
☐ Herring Gull (*Larus argentatus*)
☐ Yellow-legged Gull (*Larus cachinnans*)   91
☐ Thayer's Gull (*Larus thayeri*)

☐ Iceland Gull (*Larus glaucoides*)
☐ Lesser Black-backed Gull (*Larus fuscus*)
☐ Yellow-footed Gull (*Larus livens*)   92
☐ Western Gull (*Larus occidentalis*)
☐ Glaucous-winged Gull (*Larus glaucescens*)
☐ Glaucous Gull (*Larus hyperboreus*)
☐ Great Black-backed Gull (*Larus marinus*)   93
☐ Black-legged Kittiwake (*Rissa tridactyla*)
☐ Red-legged Kittiwake (*Rissa brevirostris*)
☐ Ross's Gull (*Rhodostethia rosea*)
☐ Sabine's Gull (*Xema sabini*)   94
☐ Ivory Gull (*Pagophila eburnea*)
☐ Gull-billed Tern (*Sterna nilotica*)
☐ Caspian Tern (*Sterna caspia*)
☐ Royal Tern (*Sterna maxima*)   95
☐ Elegant Tern (*Sterna elegans*)
☐ Sandwich Tern (*Sterna sandvicensis*)
☐ Roseate Tern (*Sterna dougallii*)
☐ Common Tern (*Sterna hirundo*)   96
☐ Arctic Tern (*Sterna paradisaea*)
☐ Forster's Tern (*Sterna forsteri*)
☐ Least Tern (*Sterna antillarum*)
☐ Bridled Tern (*Sterna anaethetus*)   101
☐ Sooty Tern (*Sterna fuscata*)
☐ White-winged Tern (*Chlidonias leucopterus*)
☐ Black Tern (*Chlidonias niger*)
☐ Brown Noddy (*Anous stolidus*)   102
☐ Black Skimmer (*Rynchops niger*)

MURRES, AUKS, AND PUFFINS (*Suborder Alcae*) 102
☐ Dovekie (*Alle alle*)
☐ Common Murre (*Uria aalge*)
☐ Thick-billed Murre (*Uria lomvia*)   103
☐ Razorbill (*Alca torda*)
☐ Black Guillemot (*Cepphus grylle*)
☐ Pigeon Guillemot (*Cepphus columba*)
☐ Marbled Murrelet
     (*Brachyramphus marmoratus*)   104
☐ Kittlitz's Murrelet
     (*Brachyramphus brevirostris*)
☐ Xantus's Murrelet
     (*Synthliboramphus hypoleucus*)
☐ Craveri's Murrelet (*Synthliboramphus craveri*)
☐ Ancient Murrelet
     (*Synthliboramphus antiquus*)   105
☐ Cassin's Auklet (*Ptychoramphus aleuticus*)

☐ Parakeet Auklet (*Cyclorrhynchus psittacula*)
☐ Least Auklet (*Aethia pusilla*)
☐ Whiskered Auklet (*Aethia pygmaea*)   106
☐ Crested Auklet (*Aethia cristatella*)
☐ Rhinoceros Auklet (*Cerorhinca monocerata*)
☐ Tufted Puffin (*Fratercula cirrhata*)
☐ Atlantic Puffin (*Fratercula arctica*)   107
☐ Horned Puffin (*Fratercula corniculata*)

PIGEONS AND DOVES (*Order Columbiformes*)   107

☐ Rock Dove (*Columba livia*)
☐ White-crowned Pigeon
     (*Columba leucocephala*)
☐ Band-tailed Pigeon (*Columba fasciata*)   108
☐ Eurasian Collared-Dove
     (*Streptopelia decaocto*)
☐ Spotted Dove (*Streptopelia chinensis*)
☐ White-winged Dove (*Zenaida asiatica*)
☐ Mourning Dove (*Zenaida macroura*)   109
☐ Inca Dove (*Columbina inca*)
☐ Common Ground-Dove
     (*Columbina passerina*)
☐ Ruddy Ground-Dove (*Columbina talpacoti*)
☐ White-tipped Dove (*Leptotila verreauxi*)   110

PARROTS (*Order Psittaciformes*)   110

☐ Budgerigar (*Melopsittacus undulatus*)
☐ Monk Parakeet (*Myiopsitta monachus*)
☐ Canary-winged Parakeet
     (*Brotogeris versicolurus*)
☐ Red-crowned Parrot
     (*Amazona viridigenalis*)   111

CUCKOOS (*Order Cuculiformes*)   111

☐ Black-billed Cuckoo (*Coccyzus erythropthalmus*)
☑ Yellow-billed Cuckoo (*Coccyzus americanus*)
☐ Mangrove Cuckoo (*Coccyzus minor*)
☐ Lesser Roadrunner (*Geococcyx velox*)   112
☐ Greater Roadrunner (*Geococcyx californianus*)
☐ Smooth-billed Ani (*Crotophaga ani*)
☐ Groove-billed Ani (*Crotophaga sulcirostris*)

OWLS (Order Strigiformes)   113

- ☐ Barn Owl (*Tyto alba*)
- ☐ Flammulated Owl (*Otus flammeolus*)
- ☐ Eastern Screech-Owl (*Otus asio*)
- ☐ Western Screech-Owl (*Otus kennicottii*)
- ☐ Whiskered Screech-Owl (*Otus trichopsis*)   114
- ☑ Great Horned Owl (*Bubo virginianus*)
- ☐ Snowy Owl (*Nyctea scandiaca*)
- ☐ Northern Hawk Owl (*Surnia ulula*)
- ☐ Northern Pygmy-Owl (*Glaucidium gnoma*)   115
- ☐ Ferruginous Pygmy-Owl
      (*Glaucidium brasilianum*)
- ☐ Elf Owl (*Micrathene whitneyi*)
- ☐ Burrowing Owl (*Speotyto cunicularia*)
- ☐ Spotted Owl (*Strix occidentalis*)   116
- ☐ Barred Owl (*Strix varia*)
- ☐ Great Gray Owl (*Strix nebulosa*)
- ☐ Long-eared Owl (*Asio otus*)
- ☐ Short-eared Owl (*Asio flammeus*)   121
- ☐ Boreal Owl (*Aegolius funereus*)
- ☐ Northern Saw-whet Owl (*Aegolius acadicus*)

NIGHTJARS (Order Caprimulgiformes)   121

- ☐ Lesser Nighthawk (*Chordeiles acutipennis*)
- ☐ Common Nighthawk (*Chordeiles minor*)   122
- ☐ Antillean Nighthawk (*Chordeiles gundlachii*)
- ☐ Pauraque (*Nyctidromus albicollis*)
- ☐ Common Poorwill (*Phalaenoptilus nuttallii*)
- ☐ Chuck-will's-widow
      (*Caprimulgus carolinensis*)   123
- ☐ Buff-collared Nightjar
      (*Caprimulgus ridgwayi*)
- ☐ Whip-poor-will (*Caprimulgus vociferus*)

SWIFTS AND HUMMINGBIRDS
    (Order Apodiformes)   123

- ☐ Black Swift (*Cypseloides niger*)
- ☐ Chimney Swift (*Chaetura pelagica*)   126
- ☐ Vaux's Swift (*Chaetura vauxi*)
- ☐ White-throated Swift (*Aeronautes saxatalis*)
- ☐ Broad-billed Hummingbird
      (*Cynanthus latirostris*)

- ☐ White-eared Hummingbird
      (*Hylocharis leucotis*)   127
- ☐ Berylline Hummingbird
      (*Amazilia beryllina*)
- ☐ Buff-bellied Hummingbird
      (*Amazilia yucatanensis*)
- ☐ Violet-crowned Hummingbird
      (*Amazilia violiceps*)
- ☐ Blue-throated Hummingbird
      (*Lampornis clemenciae*)   128
- ☐ Magnificent Hummingbird (*Eugenes fulgens*)
- ☐ Plain-capped Starthroat (*Heliomaster constantii*)
- ☐ Bahama Woodstar (*Calliphlox evelynae*)
- ☐ Lucifer Hummingbird (*Calothorax lucifer*)   129
- ☑ Ruby-throated Hummingbird
      (*Archilochus colubris*)
- ☐ Black-chinned Hummingbird
      (*Archilochus alexandri*)
- ☐ Anna's Hummingbird (*Calypte anna*)
- ☐ Costa's Hummingbird (*Calypte costae*)   130
- ☐ Calliope Hummingbird (*Stellula calliope*)
- ☐ Broad-tailed Hummingbird
      (*Selasphorus platycercus*)
- ☐ Rufous Hummingbird (*Selasphorus rufus*)
- ☐ Allen's Hummingbird (*Selasphorus sasin*)   131

TROGONS (Order Trogoniformes)   131

- ☐ Elegant Trogon (*Trogon elegans*)
- ☐ Eared Trogon (*Euptilotis neoxenus*)

KINGFISHERS (Order Coraciiformes)   131

- ☐ Ringed Kingfisher (*Ceryle torquata*)
- ☑ Belted Kingfisher (*Ceryle alcyon*)   132
- ☐ Green Kingfisher (*Chloroceryle americana*)

WOODPECKERS (Order Piciformes)   132

- ☐ Lewis's Woodpecker (*Melanerpes lewis*)
- ☑ Red-headed Woodpecker
      (*Melanerpes erythrocephalus*)
- ☐ Acorn Woodpecker (*Melanerpes formicivorus*) 133
- ☐ Gila Woodpecker (*Melanerpes uropygialis*)

- ☐ Golden-fronted Woodpecker
      (*Melanerpes aurifrons*)
- ☐ Red-bellied Woodpecker
      (*Melanerpes carolinus*)
- ☐ Yellow-bellied Sapsucker (*Sphyrapicus varius*) 134
- ☐ Red-naped Sapsucker (*Sphyrapicus nuchalis*)
- ☐ Red-breasted Sapsucker (*Sphyrapicus ruber*)
- ☐ Williamson's Sapsucker
      (*Sphyrapicus thyroideus*)
- ☐ Ladder-backed Woodpecker
      (*Picoides scalaris*)   135
- ☐ Nuttall's Woodpecker (*Picoides nuttallii*)
- ☑ Downy Woodpecker (*Picoides pubescens*)
- ☑ Hairy Woodpecker (*Picoides villosus*)
- ☐ Strickland's Woodpecker
      (*Picoides stricklandi*)   136
- ☐ Red-cockaded Woodpecker
      (*Picoides borealis*)
- ☐ White-headed Woodpecker
      (*Picoides albolarvatus*)
- ☐ Three-toed Woodpecker (*Picoides tridactylus*)
- ☐ Black-backed Woodpecker (*Picoides arcticus*) 141
- ☑ Northern Flicker (*Colaptes auratus*)
- ☐ Gilded Flicker (*Colaptes chrysoides*)
- ☑ Pileated Woodpecker (*Dryocopus pileatus*)

PERCHING BIRDS (Order Passeriformes)   142

TYRANT-FLYCATCHERS (Family Tryannidae)

- ☐ Northern Beardless-Tyrannulet
      (*Camptostoma imberbe*)
- ☐ Olive-sided Flycatcher (*Contopus borealis*)
- ☐ Greater Pewee (*Contopus pertinax*)
- ☐ Western Wood-Pewee (*Contopus sordidulus*)
- ☐ Eastern Wood-Pewee (*Contopus virens*)   143
- ☐ Yellow-bellied Flycatcher
      (*Empidonax flaviventris*)
- ☐ Acadian Flycatcher (*Empidonax virescens*)
- ☐ Alder Flycatcher (*Empidonax alnorum*)
- ☐ Willow Flycatcher (*Empidonax traillii*)   144
- ☐ Least Flycatcher (*Empidonax minimus*)
- ☐ Hammond's Flycatcher
      (*Empidonax hammondii*)
- ☐ Dusky Flycatcher (*Empidonax oberholseri*)
- ☐ Gray Flycatcher (*Empidonax wrightii*)   145

☐ Pacific-slope Flycatcher *(Empidonax difficilis)*
☐ Cordilleran Flycatcher *(Empidonax occidentalis)*
☐ Black Phoebe *(Sayornis nigricans)*
☐ Eastern Phoebe *(Sayornis phoebe)* 146
☐ Say's Phoebe *(Sayornis saya)*
☐ Vermilion Flycatcher *(Pyrocephalus rubinus)*
☐ Dusky-capped Flycatcher
    (Myiarchus tuberculifer)
☐ Ash-throated Flycatcher
    (Myiarchus cinerascens) 147
☐ Nutting's Flycatcher *(Myiarchus nuttingi)*
☐ Great Crested Flycatcher *(Myiarchus crinitus)*
☐ Brown-crested Flycatcher
    (Myiarchus tyrannulus)
☐ La Sagra's Flycatcher *(Myiarchus sagrae)* 148
☐ Great Kiskadee *(Pitangus sulphuratus)*
☐ Sulphur-bellied Flycatcher
    (Myiodynastes luteiventris)
☐ Tropical Kingbird *(Tyrannus melancholicus)*
☐ Couch's Kingbird *(Tyrannus couchii)* 149
☐ Cassin's Kingbird *(Tyrannus vociferans)*
☐ Western Kingbird *(Tyrannus verticalis)*
☒ Eastern Kingbird *(Tyrannus tyrannus)*
☐ Gray Kingbird *(Tyrannus dominicensis)* 150
☐ Loggerhead Kingbird
    (Tyrannus caudifasciatus)
☐ Scissor-tailed Flycatcher *(Tyrannus forficatus)*
☐ Fork-tailed Flycatcher *(Tyrannus savana)*
☐ Rose-throated Becard
    (Pachyramphus aglaiae) 151

LARKS *(Family Alaudidae)* 151
☐ Sky Lark *(Alauda arvensis)*
☐ Horned Lark *(Eremophila alpestris)*

SWALLOWS *(Family Hirundinidae)* 151
☐ Purple Martin *(Progne subis)*
☑ Tree Swallow *(Tachycineta bicolor)* 152
☐ Violet-green Swallow *(Tachycineta thalassina)*
☐ Bahama Swallow *(Tachycineta cyaneoviridis)*
☐ Northern Rough-winged Swallow
    (Stelgidopteryx serripennis)
☐ Bank Swallow *(Riparia riparia)* 153
☐ Cliff Swallow *(Hirundo pyrrhonota)*
☐ Cave Swallow *(Hirundo fulva)*
☐ Barn Swallow *(Hirundo rustica)*

JAYS AND CROWS *(Family Corvidae)* 154
☐ Gray Jay *(Perisoreus canadensis)*
☐ Steller's Jay *(Cyanocitta stelleri)*
☑ Blue Jay *(Cyanocitta cristata)*
☐ Green Jay *(Cyanocorax yncas)*
☐ Brown Jay *(Cyanocorax morio)* 155
☐ Florida Scrub-Jay *(Aphelocoma coerulescens)*
☐ Island Scrub-Jay *(Aphelocoma insularis)*
☐ Western Scrub-Jay *(Aphelocoma californica)*
☐ Mexican Jay *(Aphelocoma ultramarina)* 156
☐ Pinyon Jay *(Gymnorhinus cyanocephalus)*
☐ Clark's Nutcracker *(Nucifraga columbiana)*
☐ Black-billed Magpie *(Pica pica)*
☐ Yellow-billed Magpie *(Pica nuttalli)* 161
☐ American Crow *(Corvus brachyrhynchos)*
☐ Northwestern Crow *(Corvus caurinus)*
☐ Mexican Crow *(Corvus imparatus)*
☐ Fish Crow *(Corvus ossifragus)* 162
☐ Chihuahuan Raven *(Corvus cryptoleucus)*
☐ Common Raven *(Corvus corax)*

TITMICE *(Family Paridae)* 162
☑ Black-capped Chickadee *(Parus atricapillus)*
☐ Carolina Chickadee *(Parus carolinensis)* 163
☐ Mountain Chickadee *(Parus gambeli)*
☐ Siberian Tit *(Parus cinctus)*
☐ Boreal Chickadee *(Parus hudsonicus)*
☐ Chestnut-backed Chickadee
    (Parus rufescens) 164
☐ Bridled Titmouse *(Parus wollweberi)*
☐ Plain Titmouse *(Parus inornatus)*
☑ Tufted Titmouse *(Parus bicolor)*

VERDINS *(Family Remizidae)* 165
☐ Verdin *(Auriparus flaviceps)*

BUSHTITS *(Family Aegithalidae)* 165
☐ Bushtit *(Psaltriparus minimus)*

NUTHATCHES *(Family Sittidae)* 165
☑ Red-breasted Nuthatch
    (Sitta canadensis)
☐ White-breasted Nuthatch
    (Sitta carolinensis)
☐ Pygmy Nuthatch *(Sitta pygmaea)* 166
☐ Brown-headed Nuthatch *(Sitta pusilla)*

CREEPERS *(Family Certhiidae)* 166
☐ Brown Creeper *(Certhia americana)*

BULBULS *(Family Pycnonotidae)* 166
☐ Red-whiskered Bulbul *(Pycnonotus jocosus)*

WRENS *(Family Troglodytidae)* 167
☐ Cactus Wren *(Campylorhynchus brunneicapillus)*
☐ Rock Wren *(Salpinctes obsoletus)*
☐ Canyon Wren *(Catherpes mexicanus)*
☐ Carolina Wren *(Thryothorus ludovicianus)*
☐ Bewick's Wren *(Thryomanes bewickii)* 168
☑ House Wren *(Troglodytes aedon)*
☐ Winter Wren *(Troglodytes troglodytes)*
☐ Sedge Wren *(Cistothorus platensis)*
☐ Marsh Wren *(Cistothorus palustris)* 169

DIPPERS *(Family Cinclidae)* 169
☐ American Dipper *(Cinclus mexicanus)*

OLD WORLD WARBLERS AND THRUSHES
    (Family Muscicapidae) 169
☐ Arctic Warbler *(Phylloscopus borealis)*
☐ Golden-crowned Kinglet *(Regulus satrapa)*
☐ Ruby-crowned Kinglet *(Regulus calendula)* 170
☑ Blue-gray Gnatcatcher *(Polioptila caerulea)*
☐ California Gnatcatcher *(Polioptila californica)*
☐ Black-tailed Gnatcatcher *(Polioptila melanura)*
☐ Black-capped Gnatcatcher
    (Polioptila nigriceps) 172
☐ Bluethroat *(Luscinia svecica)*
☐ Northern Wheatear *(Oenanthe oenanthe)*
☑ Eastern Bluebird *(Sialia sialis)*
☐ Western Bluebird *(Sialia mexicana)* 173
☐ Mountain Bluebird *(Sialia currucoides)*
☐ Townsend's Solitaire *(Myadestes townsendi)*
☐ Veery *(Catharus fuscescens)*
☐ Gray-cheeked Thrush *(Catharus minimus)* 174
☐ Bicknell's Thrush *(Catharus bicknelli)*
☐ Swainson's Thrush *(Catharus ustulatus)*
☐ Hermit Thrush *(Catharus guttatus)*
☐ Wood Thrush *(Hylocichla mustelina)* 175
☐ Clay-colored Robin *(Turdus grayi)*
☑ American Robin *(Turdus migratorius)*
☐ Varied Thrush *(Ixoreus naevius)*
☐ Wrentit *(Chamaea fasciata)* 176

MIMIC-THRUSHES *(Family Mimidae)* 176
- [ ] Gray Catbird *(Dumetella carolinensis)*
- [ ] Northern Mockingbird *(Mimus polyglottos)*
- [ ] Sage Thrasher *(Oreoscoptes montanus)*
- [ ] Brown Thrasher *(Toxostoma rufum)* 181
- [ ] Long-billed Thrasher *(Toxostoma longirostre)*
- [ ] Bendire's Thrasher *(Toxostoma bendirei)*
- [ ] Curve-billed Thrasher *(Toxostoma curvirostre)*
- [ ] California Thrasher *(Toxostoma redivivum)* 182
- [ ] Crissal Thrasher *(Toxostoma crissale)*
- [ ] Le Conte's Thrasher *(Toxostoma lecontei)*

WAGTAILS AND PIPITS *(Family Motacillidae)* 182
- [ ] Yellow Wagtail *(Motacilla flava)*
- [ ] White Wagtail *(Motacilla alba)* 183
- [ ] Black-backed Wagtail *(Motacilla lugens)*
- [ ] Red-throated Pipit *(Anthus cervinus)*
- [ ] American Pipit *(Anthus rubescens)*
- [ ] Sprague's Pipit *(Anthus spragueii)* 184

WAXWINGS *(Family Bombycillidae)* 184
- [ ] Bohemian Waxwing *(Bombycilla garrulus)*
- [x] Cedar Waxwing *(Bombycilla cedrorum)*

SILKY-FLYCATCHERS *(Family Ptilogonatidae)* 184
- [ ] Phainopepla *(Phainopepla nitens)*

SHRIKES *(Family Laniidae)* 185
- [ ] Northern Shrike *(Lanius excubitor)*
- [ ] Loggerhead Shrike *(Lanius ludovicianus)*

STARLINGS *(Family Sturnidae)* 185
- [ ] European Starling *(Sturnus vulgaris)*
- [ ] Crested Myna *(Acridotheres cristatellus)*
- [ ] Hill Myna *(Gracula religiosa)* 186

VIREOS *(Family Vireonidae)* 186
- [ ] White-eyed Vireo *(Vireo griseus)*
- [ ] Bell's Vireo *(Vireo bellii)*
- [ ] Black-capped Vireo *(Vireo atricapillus)*
- [ ] Gray Vireo *(Vireo vicinior)* 187
- [ ] Solitary Vireo *(Vireo solitarius)*
- [ ] Yellow-throated Vireo *(Vireo flavifrons)*
- [ ] Hutton's Vireo *(Vireo huttoni)*
- [ ] Warbling Vireo *(Vireo gilvus)* 188
- [ ] Philadelphia Vireo *(Vireo philadelphicus)*

- [ ] Red-eyed Vireo *(Vireo olivaceus)*
- [ ] Black-whiskered Vireo *(Vireo altiloquus)*

WARBLERS *(Family Emberizidae)* 189

WOOD WARBLERS *(Subfamily Parulinae)*
- [ ] Blue-winged Warbler *(Vermivora pinus)*
- [ ] Golden-winged Warbler *(Vermivora chrysoptera)*
- [ ] Tennessee Warbler *(Vermivora peregrina)*
- [ ] Orange-crowned Warbler *(Vermivora celata)*
- [ ] Nashville Warbler *(Vermivora ruficapilla)* 190
- [ ] Virginia's Warbler *(Vermivora virginiae)*
- [ ] Colima Warbler *(Vermivora crissalis)*
- [ ] Lucy's Warbler *(Vermivora luciae)*
- [ ] Northern Parula *(Parula americana)* 191
- [ ] Tropical Parula *(Parula pitiayumi)*
- [ ] Yellow Warbler *(Dendroica petechia)*
- [ ] Chestnut-sided Warbler
    (Dendroica pensylvanica)
- [ ] Magnolia Warbler *(Dendroica magnolia)* 192
- [ ] Cape May Warbler *(Dendroica tigrina)*
- [ ] Black-throated Blue Warbler
    (Dendroica caerulescens)
- [ ] Yellow-rumped Warbler *(Dendroica coronata)*
- [ ] Black-throated Gray Warbler
    (Dendroica nigrescens) 193
- [ ] Townsend's Warbler *(Dendroica townsendi)*
- [ ] Hermit Warbler *(Dendroica occidentalis)*
- [ ] Black-throated Green Warbler
    (Dendroica virens)
- [ ] Golden-cheeked Warbler
    (Dendroica chrysoparia) 194
- [ ] Blackburnian Warbler *(Dendroica fusca)*
- [ ] Yellow-throated Warbler *(Dendroica dominica)*
- [ ] Grace's Warbler *(Dendroica graciae)*
- [ ] Pine Warbler *(Dendroica pinus)* 195
- [ ] Kirtland's Warbler *(Dendroica kirtlandii)*
- [ ] Prairie Warbler *(Dendroica discolor)*
- [ ] Palm Warbler *(Dendroica palmarum)*
- [ ] Bay-breasted Warbler *(Dendroica castanea)* 196
- [ ] Blackpoll Warbler *(Dendroica striata)*
- [ ] Cerulean Warbler *(Dendroica cerulea)*
- [ ] Black-and-white Warbler *(Mniotilta varia)*
- [ ] American Redstart *(Setophaga ruticilla)* 201
- [ ] Prothonotary Warbler *(Protonotaria citrea)*
- [ ] Worm-eating Warbler *(Helmitheros vermivorus)*

- [ ] Swainson's Warbler *(Limnothlypis swainsonii)*
- [ ] Ovenbird *(Seiurus aurocapillus)* 202
- [ ] Northern Waterthrush *(Seiurus noveboracensis)*
- [ ] Louisiana Waterthrush *(Seiurus motacilla)*
- [ ] Kentucky Warbler *(Oporornis formosus)*
- [ ] Connecticut Warbler *(Oporornis agilis)* 203
- [ ] Mourning Warbler *(Oporornis philadelphia)*
- [ ] MacGillivray's Warbler *(Oporornis tolmiei)*
- [x] Common Yellowthroat *(Geothlypis trichas)*
- [ ] Hooded Warbler *(Wilsonia citrina)* 204
- [ ] Wilson's Warbler *(Wilsonia pusilla)*
- [ ] Canada Warbler *(Wilsonia canadensis)*
- [ ] Red-faced Warbler *(Cardellina rubrifrons)*

TANAGERS *(Subfamily Thraupinae)* 205
- [ ] Painted Redstart *(Myioborus pictus)*
- [ ] Yellow-breasted Chat *(Icteria virens)*
- [ ] Hepatic Tanager *(Piranga flava)*
- [ ] Summer Tanager *(Piranga rubra)*
- [x] Scarlet Tanager *(Piranga olivacea)* 206
- [ ] Western Tanager *(Piranga ludoviciana)*
- [ ] Flame-colored Tanager *(Piranga bidentata)*

CARDINALS *(Subfamily Cardinalinae)* 206
- [ ] Northern Cardinal *(Cardinalis cardinalis)*
- [ ] Pyrrhuloxia *(Cardinalis sinuatus)* 207
- [ ] Rose-breasted Grosbeak
    (Pheucticus ludovicianus)
- [ ] Black-headed Grosbeak
    (Pheucticus melanocephalus)
- [ ] Blue Grosbeak *(Guiraca caerulea)*
- [ ] Lazuli Bunting *(Passerina amoena)* 208
- [x] Indigo Bunting *(Passerina cyanea)*
- [ ] Varied Bunting *(Passerina versicolor)*
- [ ] Painted Bunting *(Passerina ciris)*
- [ ] Dickcissel *(Spiza americana)* 209

NEW WORLD SPARROWS
    (Subfamily Emberizinae) 209
- [ ] Olive Sparrow *(Arremonops rufivirgatus)*
- [ ] Green-tailed Towhee *(Pipilo chlorurus)*
- [ ] Spotted Towhee *(Pipilo maculatus)*
- [x] Eastern Towhee *(Pipilo erythrophthalmus)* 210
- [ ] California Towhee *(Pipilo crissalis)*
- [ ] Canyon Towhee *(Pipilo fuscus)*
- [ ] Abert's Towhee *(Pipilo aberti)*

☐ Bachman's Sparrow (*Aimophila aestivalis*)   211
☐ Botteri's Sparrow (*Aimophila botterii*)
☐ Cassin's Sparrow (*Aimophila cassinii*)
☐ Rufous-winged Sparrow (*Aimophila carpalis*)
☐ Rufous-crowned Sparrow
    (*Aimophila ruficeps*)   212
☐ American Tree Sparrow (*Spizella arborea*)
☒ Chipping Sparrow (*Spizella passerina*)
☐ Clay-colored Sparrow (*Spizella pallida*)
☐ Brewer's Sparrow (*Spizella breweri*)   213
☐ Field Sparrow (*Spizella pusilla*)
☐ Black-chinned Sparrow (*Spizella atrogularis*)
☐ Vesper Sparrow (*Pooecetes gramineus*)
☐ Lark Sparrow (*Chondestes grammacus*)   214
☐ Black-throated Sparrow
    (*Amphispiza bilineata*)
☐ Sage Sparrow (*Amphispiza belli*)
☐ Five-striped Sparrow
    (*Amphispiza quinquestriata*)
☐ Lark Bunting (*Calamospiza melanocorys*)   215
☐ Savannah Sparrow (*Passerculus sandwichensis*)
☐ Baird's Sparrow (*Ammodramus bairdii*)
☐ Grasshopper Sparrow
    (*Ammodramus savannarum*)
☐ Henslow's Sparrow (*Ammodramus henslowii*)   216
☐ Le Conte's Sparrow (*Ammodramus leconteii*)
☐ Saltmarsh Sharp-tailed Sparrow
    (*Ammodramus caudacutus*)
☐ Nelson's Sharp-tailed Sparrow
    (*Ammodramus nelsoni*)
☐ Seaside Sparrow (*Ammodramus maritimus*)   221
☐ Fox Sparrow (*Passerella iliaca*)
☒ Song Sparrow (*Melospiza melodia*)
☐ Lincoln's Sparrow (*Melospiza lincolnii*)
☐ Swamp Sparrow (*Melospiza georgiana*)   222

☒ White-throated Sparrow
    (*Zonotrichia albicollis*)
☐ Golden-crowned Sparrow
    (*Zonotrichia atricapilla*)
☒ White-crowned Sparrow
    (*Zonotrichia leucophrys*)
☐ Harris's Sparrow (*Zonotrichia querula*)   223
☐ Dark-eyed Junco (*Junco hyemalis*)
☐ Yellow-eyed Junco (*Junco phaeonotus*)
☐ McCown's Longspur (*Calcarius mccownii*)
☐ Lapland Longspur (*Calcarius lapponicus*)   224
☐ Smith's Longspur (*Calcarius pictus*)
☐ Chestnut-collared Longspur
    (*Calcarius ornatus*)
☐ Snow Bunting (*Plectrophenax nivalis*)
☐ McKay's Bunting
    (*Plectrophenax hyperboreus*)   226

NEW WORLD BLACKBIRDS AND ORIOLES
    (Subfamily Icterinae)   226
☒ Bobolink (*Dolichonyx oryzivorus*)
☐ Red-winged Blackbird (*Agelaius phoeniceus*)
☐ Tricolored Blackbird (*Agelaius tricolor*)
☐ Eastern Meadowlark (*Sturnella magna*)   227
☐ Western Meadowlark (*Sturnella neglecta*)
☐ Yellow-headed Blackbird
    (*Xanthocephalus xanthocephalus*)
☐ Rusty Blackbird (*Euphagus carolinus*)
☐ Brewer's Blackbird (*Euphagus cyanocephalus*)   228
☐ Great-tailed Grackle (*Quiscalus mexicanus*)
☐ Boat-tailed Grackle (*Quiscalus major*)
☐ Common Grackle (*Quiscalus quiscula*)
☐ Shiny Cowbird (*Molothrus bonariensis*)   229
☐ Bronzed Cowbird (*Molothrus aeneus*)
☐ Brown-headed Cowbird (*Molothrus ater*)

☐ Orchard Oriole (*Icterus spurius*)
☐ Hooded Oriole (*Icterus cucullatus*)   230
☐ Spot-breasted Oriole (*Icterus pectoralis*)
☐ Altamira Oriole (*Icterus gularis*)
☐ Audubon's Oriole (*Icterus graduacauda*)
☒ Baltimore Oriole (*Icterus galbula*)   231
☐ Bullock's Oriole (*Icterus bullockii*)
☐ Scott's Oriole (*Icterus parisorum*)

FINCHES (*Family Fringillidae*)   231
☐ Brambling (*Fringilla montifringilla*)
☐ Gray-crowned Rosy-Finch
    (*Leucosticte tephrocotis*)   232
☐ Black Rosy-Finch (*Leucosticte atrata*)
☐ Brown-capped Rosy-Finch
    (*Leucosticte australis*)
☐ Pine Grosbeak (*Pinicola enucleator*)
☐ Purple Finch (*Carpodacus purpureus*)   233
☐ Cassin's Finch (*Carpodacus cassinii*)
☒ House Finch (*Carpodacus mexicanus*)
☐ Red Crossbill (*Loxia curvirostra*)
☐ White-winged Crossbill (*Loxia leucoptera*)   234
☐ Common Redpoll (*Carduelis flammea*)
☐ Hoary Redpoll (*Carduelis hornemanni*)
☐ Pine Siskin (*Carduelis pinus*)
☐ Lesser Goldfinch (*Carduelis psaltria*)   235
☐ Lawrence's Goldfinch (*Carduelis lawrencei*)
☒ American Goldfinch (*Carduelis tristis*)
☐ European Goldfinch (*Carduelis carduelis*)
☐ Evening Grosbeak
    (*Coccothraustes vespertinus*)   236

OLD WORLD SPARROWS (*Family Passeridae*)   236
☒ House Sparrow (*Passer domesticus*)
☐ Eurasian Tree Sparrow (*Passer montanus*)

MIMIC-THRUSHES *(Family Mimidae)* 176
☐ Gray Catbird *(Dumetella carolinensis)*
☐ Northern Mockingbird *(Mimus polyglottos)*
☐ Sage Thrasher *(Oreoscoptes montanus)*
☐ Brown Thrasher *(Toxostoma rufum)* 181
☐ Long-billed Thrasher *(Toxostoma longirostre)*
☐ Bendire's Thrasher *(Toxostoma bendirei)*
☐ Curve-billed Thrasher *(Toxostoma curvirostre)*
☐ California Thrasher *(Toxostoma redivivum)* 182
☐ Crissal Thrasher *(Toxostoma crissale)*
☐ Le Conte's Thrasher *(Toxostoma lecontei)*

WAGTAILS AND PIPITS *(Family Motacillidae)* 182
☐ Yellow Wagtail *(Motacilla flava)*
☐ White Wagtail *(Motacilla alba)* 183
☐ Black-backed Wagtail *(Motacilla lugens)*
☐ Red-throated Pipit *(Anthus cervinus)*
☐ American Pipit *(Anthus rubescens)*
☐ Sprague's Pipit *(Anthus spragueii)* 184

WAXWINGS *(Family Bombycillidae)* 184
☐ Bohemian Waxwing *(Bombycilla garrulus)*
☒ Cedar Waxwing *(Bombycilla cedrorum)*

SILKY-FLYCATCHERS *(Family Ptilogonatidae)* 184
☐ Phainopepla *(Phainopepla nitens)*

SHRIKES *(Family Laniidae)* 185
☐ Northern Shrike *(Lanius excubitor)*
☐ Loggerhead Shrike *(Lanius ludovicianus)*

STARLINGS *(Family Sturnidae)* 185
☐ European Starling *(Sturnus vulgaris)*
☐ Crested Myna *(Acridotheres cristatellus)*
☐ Hill Myna *(Gracula religiosa)* 186

VIREOS *(Family Vireonidae)* 186
☐ White-eyed Vireo *(Vireo griseus)*
☐ Bell's Vireo *(Vireo bellii)*
☐ Black-capped Vireo *(Vireo atricapillus)*
☐ Gray Vireo *(Vireo vicinior)* 187
☐ Solitary Vireo *(Vireo solitarius)*
☐ Yellow-throated Vireo *(Vireo flavifrons)*
☐ Hutton's Vireo *(Vireo huttoni)*
☐ Warbling Vireo *(Vireo gilvus)* 188
☐ Philadelphia Vireo *(Vireo philadelphicus)*

☐ Red-eyed Vireo *(Vireo olivaceus)*
☐ Black-whiskered Vireo *(Vireo altiloquus)*

WARBLERS *(Family Emberizidae)* 189

WOOD WARBLERS *(Subfamily Parulinae)*
☐ Blue-winged Warbler *(Vermivora pinus)*
☐ Golden-winged Warbler *(Vermivora chrysoptera)*
☐ Tennessee Warbler *(Vermivora peregrina)*
☐ Orange-crowned Warbler *(Vermivora celata)*
☐ Nashville Warbler *(Vermivora ruficapilla)* 190
☐ Virginia's Warbler *(Vermivora virginiae)*
☐ Colima Warbler *(Vermivora crissalis)*
☐ Lucy's Warbler *(Vermivora luciae)*
☐ Northern Parula *(Parula americana)* 191
☐ Tropical Parula *(Parula pitiayumi)*
☐ Yellow Warbler *(Dendroica petechia)*
☐ Chestnut-sided Warbler
    (Dendroica pensylvanica)
☐ Magnolia Warbler *(Dendroica magnolia)* 192
☐ Cape May Warbler *(Dendroica tigrina)*
☐ Black-throated Blue Warbler
    (Dendroica caerulescens)
☐ Yellow-rumped Warbler *(Dendroica coronata)*
☐ Black-throated Gray Warbler
    (Dendroica nigrescens) 193
☐ Townsend's Warbler *(Dendroica townsendi)*
☐ Hermit Warbler *(Dendroica occidentalis)*
☐ Black-throated Green Warbler
    (Dendroica virens)
☐ Golden-cheeked Warbler
    (Dendroica chrysoparia) 194
☐ Blackburnian Warbler *(Dendroica fusca)*
☐ Yellow-throated Warbler *(Dendroica dominica)*
☐ Grace's Warbler *(Dendroica graciae)*
☐ Pine Warbler *(Dendroica pinus)* 195
☐ Kirtland's Warbler *(Dendroica kirtlandii)*
☐ Prairie Warbler *(Dendroica discolor)*
☐ Palm Warbler *(Dendroica palmarum)*
☐ Bay-breasted Warbler *(Dendroica castanea)* 196
☐ Blackpoll Warbler *(Dendroica striata)*
☐ Cerulean Warbler *(Dendroica cerulea)*
☐ Black-and-white Warbler *(Mniotilta varia)*
☐ American Redstart *(Setophaga ruticilla)* 201
☐ Prothonotary Warbler *(Protonotaria citrea)*
☐ Worm-eating Warbler *(Helmitheros vermivorus)*

☐ Swainson's Warbler *(Limnothlypis swainsonii)*
☐ Ovenbird *(Seiurus aurocapillus)* 202
☐ Northern Waterthrush *(Seiurus noveboracensis)*
☐ Louisiana Waterthrush *(Seiurus motacilla)*
☐ Kentucky Warbler *(Oporornis formosus)*
☐ Connecticut Warbler *(Oporornis agilis)* 203
☐ Mourning Warbler *(Oporornis philadelphia)*
☐ MacGillivray's Warbler *(Oporornis tolmiei)*
☒ Common Yellowthroat *(Geothlypis trichas)*
☐ Hooded Warbler *(Wilsonia citrina)* 204
☐ Wilson's Warbler *(Wilsonia pusilla)*
☐ Canada Warbler *(Wilsonia canadensis)*
☐ Red-faced Warbler *(Cardellina rubrifrons)*

TANAGERS *(Subfamily Thraupinae)* 205
☐ Painted Redstart *(Myioborus pictus)*
☐ Yellow-breasted Chat *(Icteria virens)*
☐ Hepatic Tanager *(Piranga flava)*
☐ Summer Tanager *(Piranga rubra)*
☒ Scarlet Tanager *(Piranga olivacea)* 206
☐ Western Tanager *(Piranga ludoviciana)*
☐ Flame-colored Tanager *(Piranga bidentata)*

CARDINALS *(Subfamily Cardinalinae)* 206
☐ Northern Cardinal *(Cardinalis cardinalis)*
☐ Pyrrhuloxia *(Cardinalis sinuatus)* 207
☐ Rose-breasted Grosbeak
    (Pheucticus ludovicianus)
☐ Black-headed Grosbeak
    (Pheucticus melanocephalus)
☐ Blue Grosbeak *(Guiraca caerulea)*
☐ Lazuli Bunting *(Passerina amoena)* 208
☒ Indigo Bunting *(Passerina cyanea)*
☐ Varied Bunting *(Passerina versicolor)*
☐ Painted Bunting *(Passerina ciris)*
☐ Dickcissel *(Spiza americana)* 209

NEW WORLD SPARROWS
    (Subfamily Emberizinae) 209
☐ Olive Sparrow *(Arremonops rufivirgatus)*
☐ Green-tailed Towhee *(Pipilo chlorurus)*
☐ Spotted Towhee *(Pipilo maculatus)*
☒ Eastern Towhee *(Pipilo erythrophthalmus)* 210
☐ California Towhee *(Pipilo crissalis)*
☐ Canyon Towhee *(Pipilo fuscus)*
☐ Abert's Towhee *(Pipilo aberti)*

☐ Bachman's Sparrow (*Aimophila aestivalis*) 211
☐ Botteri's Sparrow (*Aimophila botterii*)
☐ Cassin's Sparrow (*Aimophila cassinii*)
☐ Rufous-winged Sparrow (*Aimophila carpalis*)
☐ Rufous-crowned Sparrow
  (*Aimophila ruficeps*) 212
☐ American Tree Sparrow (*Spizella arborea*)
☒ Chipping Sparrow (*Spizella passerina*)
☐ Clay-colored Sparrow (*Spizella pallida*)
☐ Brewer's Sparrow (*Spizella breweri*) 213
☐ Field Sparrow (*Spizella pusilla*)
☐ Black-chinned Sparrow (*Spizella atrogularis*)
☐ Vesper Sparrow (*Pooecetes gramineus*)
☐ Lark Sparrow (*Chondestes grammacus*) 214
☐ Black-throated Sparrow
  (*Amphispiza bilineata*)
☐ Sage Sparrow (*Amphispiza belli*)
☐ Five-striped Sparrow
  (*Amphispiza quinquestriata*)
☐ Lark Bunting (*Calamospiza melanocorys*) 215
☐ Savannah Sparrow (*Passerculus sandwichensis*)
☐ Baird's Sparrow (*Ammodramus bairdii*)
☐ Grasshopper Sparrow
  (*Ammodramus savannarum*)
☐ Henslow's Sparrow (*Ammodramus henslowii*) 216
☐ Le Conte's Sparrow (*Ammodramus leconteii*)
☐ Saltmarsh Sharp-tailed Sparrow
  (*Ammodramus caudacutus*)
☐ Nelson's Sharp-tailed Sparrow
  (*Ammodramus nelsoni*)
☐ Seaside Sparrow (*Ammodramus maritimus*) 221
☐ Fox Sparrow (*Passerella iliaca*)
☒ Song Sparrow (*Melospiza melodia*)
☐ Lincoln's Sparrow (*Melospiza lincolnii*)
☐ Swamp Sparrow (*Melospiza georgiana*) 222

☒ White-throated Sparrow
  (*Zonotrichia albicollis*)
☐ Golden-crowned Sparrow
  (*Zonotrichia atricapilla*)
☒ White-crowned Sparrow
  (*Zonotrichia leucophrys*)
☐ Harris's Sparrow (*Zonotrichia querula*) 223
☐ Dark-eyed Junco (*Junco hyemalis*)
☐ Yellow-eyed Junco (*Junco phaeonotus*)
☐ McCown's Longspur (*Calcarius mccownii*)
☐ Lapland Longspur (*Calcarius lapponicus*) 224
☐ Smith's Longspur (*Calcarius pictus*)
☐ Chestnut-collared Longspur
  (*Calcarius ornatus*)
☐ Snow Bunting (*Plectrophenax nivalis*)
☐ McKay's Bunting
  (*Plectrophenax hyperboreus*) 226

NEW WORLD BLACKBIRDS AND ORIOLES
  (Subfamily *Icterinae*) 226
☒ Bobolink (*Dolichonyx oryzivorus*)
☐ Red-winged Blackbird (*Agelaius phoeniceus*)
☐ Tricolored Blackbird (*Agelaius tricolor*)
☐ Eastern Meadowlark (*Sturnella magna*) 227
☐ Western Meadowlark (*Sturnella neglecta*)
☐ Yellow-headed Blackbird
  (*Xanthocephalus xanthocephalus*)
☐ Rusty Blackbird (*Euphagus carolinus*)
☐ Brewer's Blackbird (*Euphagus cyanocephalus*) 228
☐ Great-tailed Grackle (*Quiscalus mexicanus*)
☐ Boat-tailed Grackle (*Quiscalus major*)
☐ Common Grackle (*Quiscalus quiscula*)
☐ Shiny Cowbird (*Molothrus bonariensis*) 229
☐ Bronzed Cowbird (*Molothrus aeneus*)
☐ Brown-headed Cowbird (*Molothrus ater*)

☐ Orchard Oriole (*Icterus spurius*)
☐ Hooded Oriole (*Icterus cucullatus*) 230
☐ Spot-breasted Oriole (*Icterus pectoralis*)
☐ Altamira Oriole (*Icterus gularis*)
☐ Audubon's Oriole (*Icterus graduacauda*)
☒ Baltimore Oriole (*Icterus galbula*) 231
☐ Bullock's Oriole (*Icterus bullockii*)
☐ Scott's Oriole (*Icterus parisorum*)

FINCHES (Family *Fringillidae*) 231
☐ Brambling (*Fringilla montifringilla*)
☐ Gray-crowned Rosy-Finch
  (*Leucosticte tephrocotis*) 232
☐ Black Rosy-Finch (*Leucosticte atrata*)
☐ Brown-capped Rosy-Finch
  (*Leucosticte australis*)
☐ Pine Grosbeak (*Pinicola enucleator*)
☐ Purple Finch (*Carpodacus purpureus*) 233
☐ Cassin's Finch (*Carpodacus cassinii*)
☒ House Finch (*Carpodacus mexicanus*)
☐ Red Crossbill (*Loxia curvirostra*)
☐ White-winged Crossbill (*Loxia leucoptera*) 234
☐ Common Redpoll (*Carduelis flammea*)
☐ Hoary Redpoll (*Carduelis hornemanni*)
☐ Pine Siskin (*Carduelis pinus*)
☐ Lesser Goldfinch (*Carduelis psaltria*) 235
☐ Lawrence's Goldfinch (*Carduelis lawrencei*)
☒ American Goldfinch (*Carduelis tristis*)
☐ European Goldfinch (*Carduelis carduelis*)
☐ Evening Grosbeak
  (*Coccothraustes vespertinus*) 236

OLD WORLD SPARROWS (Family *Passeridae*) 236
☒ House Sparrow (*Passer domesticus*)
☐ Eurasian Tree Sparrow (*Passer montanus*)

PHOTOGRAPHY CREDITS

FRONT COVER: Western Tanager, Scarlet Tanager by John James Audubon, Courtesy of the National Audubon Society

BACK COVER: Say's Phoebe, Western Kingbird, Scissor-tailed Flycatcher by John James Audubon, Courtesy of the National Audubon Society

ESSAY ILLUSTRATIONS:
Color:
Page 17: Anna's Hummingbird © Brian E. Small; Page 18: Clockwise from upper left: Summer Tanager © Tom Vezo, Great Egret © John Cancalosi, Greater Flamingo © Tim Fitzharris, Snowy Owl © Tom Vezo, Painted Bunting © Tom Vezo, Mallard © Arthur Morris/Birds As Art, Scarlet Macaw © Whit Bronaugh, House Finch © Sharon Cummings, Peacock © D. Robert Franz; Page 20: Wood Duck © Arthur Morris/Birds As Art

Courtship:
Page 37: Hummingbirds and Orchids by Martin Johnson Heade © Art Resource, New York; Page 38: Great Blue Herons © Arthur Morris/Birds As Art; Page 40: Top: Rufous-naped Lark © Stan Osolinski, Center: Magnificent Frigatebird © John Cancalosi, Bottom: Tufted Puffin © Arthur Morris/Birds As Art

Nests:
Page 57: Eastern Meadowlark by John James Audubon, Courtesy of the National Audubon Society; Page 58: American Oystercatcher © Tom Vezo, American Coot © D. Robert Franz; Page 59: Northern Gannets © Dominique Braud, Eared Grebe © Tim Fitzharris; Page 60: Osprey © D. Robert Franz, Rose-ringed Parakeet © Stan Osolinski

Eggs:
Page 77: Great-tailed Grackle eggs © Steve Bentsen; Page 78: Clockwise from upper left: Common Loon © Bill Marchel, Killdeer © John Cancalosi, Song Sparrow nest © Bill Marchel, Common Murre © Arthur Morris/Birds As Art; Page 80: Blue-footed Booby © Tom Vezo

Wings in the Wind:
Page 97: Reddish Egret © Tim Fitzharris; Page 98: American Avocet © Arthur Morris/Birds As Art; Page 100: Broad-tailed Hummingbird © Tim Fitzharris

The Bird in Mythology:
Page 117: Northern Hawk Owl © Johann Schumacher; Page 118: Clockwise from upper left: Scene with Bathers © Scala/Art Resource, Dove with Olive Twig © Eric Lessing/Art Resource, New York, Leda and the Swan © Scala/Art Resource, Birds in Papyrus Marsh © Werner Forman/Art Resource, New York; Page 120: American Crow by John James Audubon, Courtesy of the National Audubon Society

Vision:
Page 137: Tricolored Heron © Arthur Morris/Birds As Art; Page 138: Burrowing Owls © Daniel J. Cox/Natural Exposures.com; Page 139: Left: Wood Duck © Bill Marchel, Center: Brown Pelican © Tom Vezo, Right: Osprey © Tom Vezo

Song:
Page 157: Least Tern Chick © Arthur Morris/Birds As Art; Page 158: Clockwise from upper left: Yellow-headed Blackbird © D. Robert Franz, Chestnut-collared Longspur © Brian E. Small, Arctic Warbler © Tom Vezo, Western Meadowlark © Brian E. Small, Yellow Warbler © John Heidecker, White-throated Sparrow © Tom Vezo, Common Yellowthroat © Arthur Morris/Birds As Art, Red-winged Blackbird © Sharon Cummings, House Wren © Tim Fitzharris

Migration:
Page 177: Snow Geese © Arthur Morris/Birds As Art; Page 178: Arctic Tern by John James Audubon, Courtesy of the National Audubon Society; Page 180: Brown Pelicans © Tim Fitzharris

The Nocturnal World:
Page 197: Red-winged Blackbird © Johann Schumacher; Page 199: Black Rail by John James Audubon, Courtesy of the National Audubon Society; Page 200: Great Horned Owl © Tim Fitzharris

The Bird in Art:
Page 217: Wheatfield with Crows by Vincent van Gogh © Art Resource, New York; Page 218: Tree with Birds by Aaron Birnbaum © K.S. Art/Art Resource, New York; Page 219: Landscape with Swallows © Nimatallah/Art Resource, New York; Page 220: White Heron landing behind irises by Ando Hiroshige © Victoria & Albert Museum, London/Art Resource, New York

The Dinosaur Debate:
Page 237: Marabou Stork © Tim Fitzharris; Page: 238: Roseate Spoonbills © Arthur Morris/Birds As Art; Page 240: Sinosauropteryx prima © Chen Pei-ji/Nanjing Institute of Geology and Palaeontology

JOURNAL-ENTRY ILLUSTRATIONS:
Page 5: Watercolor eggs © Robbin L. Gourley; Page 13: Albatross nesting © The Granger Collection, New York; Page 23: Courtesy of The New York Public Library; Page 24: Courtesy of The New York Public Library; Page 27: Courtesy of The New York Public Library; Page 31: Flamingo and Jabiru © The Granger Collection, New York; Page 34: Chinese Teal © The Granger Collection, New York; Page 56: Satin Bowerbird © The Granger Collection, New York; Pages 62 & 63: Courtesy of The New York Public Library; Page 65: Nightingale © The Granger Collection, New York; Page 67: Rail by Alexander Wilson © The Granger Collection, New York; Page 69: Crane © The Granger Collection, New York; Page 86: Woodcock by Alexander Wilson © The Granger Collection, New York; Page 101: Designs for a Flying Machine by Leonardo Da Vinci © The Granger Collection, New York; Page 125: Wing of a Roller by Albrecht Dürer © Graphische Sammlung Albertina, Russia/Art Resource, New York; Page 141: Plate from "Avium Vivae Icones" by Adriaen Collaert © Victoria & Albert Museum, London/Art Resource, New York; Page 171: Watercolor egg © Robbin L. Gourley; Page 173: Spotted Bowerbird © The Granger Collection, New York; Page 175: Ibis © The Granger Collection, New York; Page 225: Watercolor eggs © Robbin L. Gourley; Page 227: Meadowlark © The Granger Collection, New York; Page 228: Satin Bowerbird © The Granger Collection, New York; Page 236: Bird Skeleton © The Granger Collection, New York

CONTRIBUTORS

FRED BAUMGARTEN ("The Nocturnal World") is national coordinator of National Audubon Society's Important Bird Areas Project. He is a birder, writer, and conservationist. He lives on a bucolic Audubon sanctuary in northwest Connecticut with his wife, Jenny Hansell, and their cat, Ursula.

SUSAN RONEY DRENNAN ("Nests"; "Wings in the Wind") is the former Vice President of Ornithology, National Audubon Society. She is the author of *Where to Find Birds in New York State* (Syracuse University Press, 1981).

VALERIE HARMS ("The Bird in Mythology"; "The Bird in Art") is the author of eight books, including *National Audubon Society's Almanac of the Environment: The Ecology of Everyday Life*. She is the former Project Editor of Audubon's Science Division.

STEPHEN W. KRESS ("Courtship"; "Eggs"; "Migration") is Director of National Audubon Society's Seabird Restoration Program and Manager of Audubon's Maine Coast Sanctuaries. He is author of several Audubon books, including *The Bird Garden* (Dorling Kindersley, 1995) and *Project Puffin* (Tilbury House, 1997).

GEOFFREY S. LEBARON ("Vision") is an ornithologist who has held the position of Christmas Bird Count Editor with National Audubon Society for more than ten years. Currently, he is also involved with the development of BirdSource, an on-line clearinghouse containing both historical and real-time bird information. He also leads natural history tours, and his travels have taken him to Antarctica, Australia, and across the Western Hemisphere.

VIRGINIA MORELL ("The Dinosaur Debate") is a contributing correspondent at *Science*, a contributing editor at *Discover*, and author of *Ancestral Passions* (Simon and Schuster, 1995), a biography of the Leakey family of anthropologists. Her article "The Origin of Birds: The Dinosaur Debate" appeared in the March–April 1997 issue of *Audubon* magazine.

VINCENT MUEHTER ("Color"; "Song") is Associate Director of Conservation, National Audubon Society. His chief priority is developing and implementing an innovative national bird conservation strategy for at-risk bird species. He has written articles that have been published in various peer-reviewed scientific journals, including *Birds of North America* and *Behavioral Ecology and Sociobiology*.

PHOTOGRAPHY CREDITS